Professional English

D0164852

English for the Humanities

Kristin L. Johannsen

THOMSON

Australia • Canada • México • Singapore • United Kingdom • United States

English for the Humanities

Kristin L. Johannsen

Publisher, Global ELT: Christopher Wenger
Director of Content Development: Anita Raducanu
Director of Product Marketing: Amy Mabley
Editorial Manager: Berta de Llano
International Marketing Manager: Ian Martin
Development Editor: Margarita Matte
Editorial Assistant: Bridget McLaughlin
Associate Production Editor: Erika Hokanson
Senior Print Buyer: Mary Beth Hennebury

Project Manager: Chrystie Hopkins
Photo Researcher: Alejandra Camarillo
Illustrator: Ignacio (Iñaki) Ochoa Bilbao
Interior Design/Composition: Miriam Gómez Alvarado, Israel Muñoz Olmos
Cover Design: Miriam Gómez Alvarado
Printer: Edwards Brothers

For permission to use material from this text or product,
submit a request online at http://www.thomsonrights.com

Any additional questions about permissions can be
submitted by email to thomsonrights@thomson.com

ISBN 10: 1-4130-2052-6
ISBN 13: 978-1-4130-2052-6

Library of Congress Control Number: 2006902790

For more information contact Thomson ELT, 25 Thomson
Place, Boston, Massachusetts 02210 USA, or visit our
Internet site at elt.thomson.com

Cover Photo Credits:
© Medioimages / Alamy, (top right) © Design Pics Inc. / Alamy,
(bottom left) © Brian Atkinson / Alamy, (bottom right) © Brand X
Pictures / Alamy

Photo Credits:
Photo.com RF: p17, p 18, p 20, p23, p25, p 28, p 29, p 41, p 42,
p 43, p 57, p 60, p 63,

Alamy.com RF: p 1 © Comstock Images / Alamy, p 2 © Comstock
Images / Alamy p 4 © Comstock Images / Alamy p 8 © Comstock
Images / Alamy, p 15 © Visual Arts Library (London) / Alamy, p58 ©
Blend Images / Alamy, p67 © Comstock Images / Alamy

Hemera photo objects: p 14, p 30, p 35, p 44, p 45, p 55, p 56

Contents

To the Teacher

English for the Humanities is especially designed for university students at the intermediate level who want to use their English for international communication in professional contexts.

Objective

The purpose of this book is to empower students with the language and life skills they need to carry out their career goals. To this end it provides ample opportunities for students to build awareness and practice the language in real-life scenarios. Its integrated skills approach develops the student's self-confidence to survive and succeed in professional and social encounters within an English-speaking global community.

Content

The book has been designed with a core of 30 lessons plus additional resource sections to provide teachers and course designers with the necessary flexibility for planning a wide variety of courses.

The four skills of listening, speaking, writing and reading are developed throughout each unit within professional contexts. Emphasis is on developing the life skills students need to deal with situations that they will encounter in the job market.

University students, regardless of their major, will immediately be motivated by the opportunity to prepare for the job market as they practice their English language skills in the following scenarios.

Philosophy

Graduate school, academic English, reading course catalogues, taking lecture notes, research on business ethics, formal vs informal English.

Language

Developing job interview skills, listening to instructions, business interaction, obtaining relevant information, issues in translation

Art

Craft vs art, setting up a program to help artisans sell their work, meetings and negotiations, agreeing and disagreeing politely, making suggestions, writing descriptions for promotional brochures

History

Doing volunteer work in an international project, restoring a historical site, planning an interpretive center, narrating a sequence of events, practice of the language for cooperating and organizing

Social Science

Activities of an NGO, asking survey questions in an interview, making travel plans, and making requests

Using the book

Each content-based unit is divided into six two-page lessons. Each lesson is designed to present, develop and practice job-related skills. (See **Content**.)

Vocabulary

A section with additional content vocabulary for the Humanities is included for reference. Teachers may choose to focus on this vocabulary through direct presentation, or may encourage the students to use this section for self-study.

Grammar

There is no direct grammar instruction in the core lessons. However a complete grammar resource has been provided at the end of the book. The grammar resource can serve as a reinforcement of the student's grammar skills. It can be used for self-study or independent practice or the teacher may choose to use material in class to present and practice language skills required by the productive exercises in the different lessons.

The language elements are ordered as they appear in the units. But they may be referred to in any order. Each grammar presentation provides a *grammar box* or paradigm followed by contextual examples and a practice exercise.

Listening

Many of the workplace scenarios are presented and/or established through the listening contexts. Complete audio scripts and an audio CD have been provided for the student to allow for independent listening practice. Student access to audio scripts and CDs also provides multi-level instruction opportunities in the classroom.

Ongoing Assessment

The five team projects found at the end of every unit, as well as the one-page unit reviews at the end of the book provide ample opportunity for ongoing assessment. Unit tests are provided in the Teacher's Resource Book.

Unit 1

Philosophy

Unit 1
Lesson 1

Are you going to be a philosopher

a Rafael is a new international student at Southland University. He's talking to his neighbor in the student apartments. Listen to their conversation and complete the notes.

CD T-1

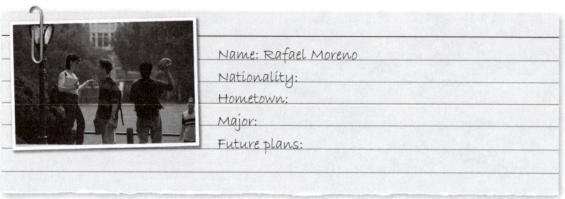

Name: Rafael Moreno
Nationality:
Hometown:
Major:
Future plans:

b Listen to the conversation again and answer these questions. Then discuss your answers with a partner.

CD T-2

1. What are two useful things that people can learn by studying philosophy?

2. How has Rafael used these things already?

3. What will he do after graduation?

4. What's your major?

5. What useful things can you learn with this major?

6. What do you hope to do after graduation?

c Rafael has received this notice for new students. Read it and find the words for the definitions on page 3.

SOUTHLAND UNIVERSITY
OFFICE OF INTERNATIONAL STUDENTS

Welcome to the university! Registration Week is September 1-7. During this time, all international students must:
- obtain a student ID card ✓ *Tuesday*
- pay tuition and fees ✓ *Tuesday*
- meet with your advisor *appointment next Monday*
- register for classes ✓ *Wednesday*
- buy textbooks *need more money! e-mailed Father*
- fill out forms at the Student Health Clinic ✓
- attend an orientation meeting for new students *Friday 3:00*
Please contact us if you need assistance with any of these steps.

1. money you pay for education _____
2. put your name on an official list _____
3. a card with your name and photo _____
4. books used for study _____
5. a medical office _____
6. a teacher who gives you advice _____
7. preparation for a new job or course of study _____

d Rafael is telling his neighbor about what he's done. Listen and fill in the verbs.

CD
T-3

1. I _____ a student ID card. I _____ it on Tuesday.

2. I _____ with my advisor yet, but I _____ an appointment.

3. I _____ a lot of forms with information about my health.

e Complete the sentences with the correct form of the verb in the *simple past* or *present perfect*.

1. He _____ (buy, not) his textbooks yet because he didn't have enough money, but he _____ (send) an e-mail to his father to ask for more.

2. He _____ (pay) all his tuition and fees, though.

3. He _____ (register) for his classes. He _____ (do) that on Wednesday.

4. He _____ (attend, not) an orientation meeting yet.

f Ask your partner questions with *Have you ever . . . ?* Add your own ideas to the list. Ask follow-up questions to get more information.

> *Have you ever taken a philosophy class? What did you learn about?*

	Yes	No	Additional information
1. take a philosophy class	☐	☐	_____
2. move to a new city	☐	☐	_____
3. have a job during vacation	☐	☐	_____
4. work with a family member	☐	☐	_____
5. _____	☐	☐	_____
6. _____	☐	☐	_____

g Discuss these questions in groups.

1. What are some questions that philosophers talk about?

2. Are you interested in philosophy? Why or why not?

3. Can philosophy be useful in daily life? If yes, how?

Lesson 2

First day of class

a Rafael just got his class schedule. With a partner, work out the meaning of the abbreviations in the schedule.

SCHEDULE

Name: MORENO, RAFAEL
ID#: 2090733   Major: Philosophy

Course	Title	Day	Time	Instr	Room
PHIL 380	Business Ethics	MWF	7:45a	Wolinsky	406 Main
PHIL 240	20th Century Philosophy	TTh	7:45a	Barker	312 Main
PHIL 450	Philosophy of Science	WF	4:15p	Pak	103 North
ENGL 217	ESL Writing	MTWTh	2:15p	Millham	24 Weston
MUSI 101	Introduction to Music History	TTh	6:15p	Dawes	Auditorium

b Look at the schedule and complete Rafael's conversation with his neighbor.

Sandy: So, how's your schedule?

Rafael: It's awful! I have to get up early (1) _____ days a week. My first class starts at (2) _____.

Sandy: Well, maybe you can go back to sleep after that.

Rafael: I guess so . . . My next class isn't until (3) _____.

Sandy: How many classes are you taking?

Rafael: (4) _____. I have three (5) _____ classes, and I also have (6) _____ four days a week.

Sandy: That sounds like a tough schedule . . . What's your other class?

Rafael: Music History. I needed one more humanities class, and that sounded interesting. I can listen to music (7) _____ a week, and the time is good. It's in the (8) _____.

c Tell a partner about your class schedule. Do you like it? Why or why not? What is the perfect class schedule?

d What do teachers often talk about on the first day of class? It's Rafael's first day in Professor Wolinsky's class in Business Ethics. List things that you think the professor will talk about.

_____   _____
_____   _____
_____   _____

e Listen to the first part of the lecture and find this information.

CD T-4

1. the professor's first name _____

2. the professor's office room number _____

3. the professor's office hours _____

4. the title of the textbook _____

f Now listen to the second part of the lecture and fill in the missing words.

CD T-5

Now, first of all, what does "business ethics" mean? And why do we (1) _____ business ethics? As you all know, ethics-and business ethics-is a branch of philosophy. The English word *philosophy* comes from the Greek.

(2) _____ for "love" and "wisdom." For the ancient Greeks, philosophy was the love of wisdom. But we need to be more specific to (3) _____ what philosophers do today.

We can say that philosophy is an area of inquiry. In it, we try to discover truths about the (4) _____ —a kind of research. In some ways, philosophy is similar to science, journalism, and detective work. All of these things try to find out what is true. But philosophy is different, because the questions it asks are more (5) _____, and more important. It asks questions about God, knowledge, the mind, and what's right and wrong. Philosophy looks into the most important (6) _____ that face all of us.

Ethics is an area of philosophy that asks a very special question. What makes an (7) _____ good or bad? This question comes up in all parts of our lives, and that includes the business world. In this course, we will talk about issues that affect you as a (8) _____, as an employer or employee, and as a consumer.

What does it *mean* to do the right thing, in a business setting? *That* is the question that we will try to answer in this class.

g The last part of the lecture talks about an ethics issue in a company. Read the statements. Then listen to the lecture and circle *T* for *True* or *F* for *False*.

CD T-6

1. Arden Textile makes clothes for sports.   T   F

2. The company's biggest factory was destroyed in a fire.   T   F

3. The company decided to build a new factory in China.   T   F

4. The company's workers received no pay for many months.   T   F

5. This decision was good for the workers.   T   F

6. This decision was good for the company.   T   F

7. The Prime Minister gave the company an award.   T   F

8. Everyone agreed with the company's decision.   T   F

h In your opinion, did the company do the right thing? Why or why not?

Lesson 3

In my opinion . . .

a The students are having a discussion in Rafael's Business Ethics class. Read their conversation. Find additional expressions and add them to the chart.

Rafael: Let's see, here's the first discussion topic. "A company's most important responsibility is to protect the environment." How do you feel about that?

Li: Personally, I think that idea is too extreme. In my country, we need to think about earning money first.

Cathy: Really? Why do you say that?

Li: Because many people don't have jobs, and we need more industry. In the future, when the country is developed and everyone has a job, then we can think about the environment.

Rafael: But it might be too late to think about the environment then.

Cathy: As I see it, businesses can protect the environment and make money at the same time.

Li: Yes, that might be true in some cases.

Asking for opinions	Giving opinions	Asking for explanations
What do you think about . . . What's your opinion of . . . Do you think that . . . _____	In my opinion, . . . It seems to me . . . As I see it, . . . _____	Why do you feel that way? What do you mean by . . . Can you explain . . . _____

b Read the survey. Give answers that are true for you.

ethics in daily life
Is it OK to . . .

1. buy copies of designer products like watches and clothes?	yes	no	sometimes
2. read a whole magazine in the store without buying it?	yes	no	sometimes
3. use an article from the Internet in a class assignment, and say your wrote it?	yes	no	sometimes
4. keep money that you found in the street?	yes	no	sometimes
5. avoid paying taxes?	yes	no	sometimes
6. buy a jacket, wear it once, and then return it to the store?	yes	no	sometimes
7. make copies of CDs or software for your friends?	yes	no	sometimes

c With your partner, take turns choosing topics from Exercise **b**. Discuss your opinions, and ask for explanations.

d Choose one topic from Exercise **b** that you and your partner have similar opinions about. Get together with another pair and see if their opinions are similar or different. Find out their reasons.

e In groups of four, read the following article and discuss the situations. Each group member should take one of the roles. Change roles after each situation.

Roles in group discussions

Leader: makes sure the group completes the activity, starts and ends the activity, and asks for ideas from every member of the group

Summarizer: explains the activity and makes sure all group members understand what to do

Secretary: writes notes on the group's ideas

Reporter: presents the group's ideas to the whole class

Ask Dr. Ethics

Ethics isn't just a class in universities. Have you ever been in situations like these? Compare your ideas with the advice we got from Dr. Ethics.

Situation 1

There's a big concert next week, and my favorite group is playing. The theater is very small so there weren't many tickets for sale. I was really lucky and got one ticket for $20. But now I don't have enough money to pay my bills this month! My friend really wants to go to the concert, and he says he'll buy my ticket at any price. Can I sell him my ticket for $40?

Situation 2

I've worked as a secretary in a big international company for the last six years. The job is OK, but my salary is really very low compared to similar jobs at other companies. The good thing about my job is that I'm not very busy in the afternoon, so I like to make phone calls to my sister and my friends when I don't have any work to do. My sister doesn't like that though, because she says I'm stealing from the company. Am I?

Situation 3

I'm an English teacher at a language institute for business people. Many of my students will get a promotion in their company if they receive a good grade in my class. Every year, some students give me presents for the holidays. These are usually small things like candy or a CD. My students know that this doesn't influence their grades for the course, but the other teachers say I shouldn't accept presents from students. What do you think?

Situation 4

I want to sell my car. It's very small and my wife and I just had a baby, so we really need a bigger car for the three of us. I was in a bad accident with the car last year. I paid more than $2000 for repairs, and the car runs well now. You can't see any damage on the car. When people come to look at my car for sale, do I have to tell them about the accident?

Dr. Ethics says . . .

 f Take turns presenting your group's answers and reasons to the class. Each student should present one situation. Use the tips in the box to help you.

Speaking to an audience

- Stand up and speak in a voice that's slightly louder than normal so that everyone can hear you.
- Use notes to help you remember the important points, but don't just read your ideas from the paper.
- Look at different people as you speak. This eye contact will make your listeners more interested in what you're saying.

Lesson 4

Too much to do

a Rafael has homework in all his classes. Listen to the professors and write down the assignments.

CD
T-7

1. Business Ethics: _____
   _____ Due _____

2. Greek and Roman Philosophy: _____
   _____ Due _____

3. ESL Writing: _____
   _____ Due _____

4. Music History: _____
   _____ Due _____

b Write sentences in your notebook about Rafael's assignments using the verbs below.

1. have to	2. should	3. not have to	4. can

 c Read the conversations with a partner, noting the underlined expressions. Then answer the questions.

Conversation 1

Rafael: Hey, Jeff. <u>Are you busy</u>?

Jeff: No. <u>What's up</u>?

Rafael: <u>Sorry for missing</u> your party last night. I just had too much to do. I have to write a paper for class, and it takes me a really long time.

Jeff: Oh, <u>that's too bad</u>! Would you like me to read your paper? I could check your English.

Rafael: That would be great! <u>Thanks</u>!

Jeff: <u>No problem</u>.

Conversation 2

Rafael: Excuse me, Dr. Barker. Do you have a moment?

Dr. Barker: Of course, Rafael. Come in. What can I do for you?

Rafael: I'm really sorry that I missed the lecture yesterday. I had to study for a test in another class.

Dr. Barker: That's unfortunate. I covered some important topics in the lecture.

Rafael: Is there anything I can do?

Dr. Barker: You could borrow lecture notes from one of your classmates. And read Chapter 3 in this book. It has a good summary.

Rafael: Thank you for your help.

Dr. Barker: Don't mention it.

1. What's the difference between the two conversations?

2. What is the reason for this difference?

d Write the expressions from Conversation 2 that have the same meanings.

1. Are you busy? _____
2. What's up? _____
3. Sorry for missing _____

4. That's too bad. _____
5. Thanks. _____
6. No problem. _____

e Work with a partner to make this conversation more polite.

Student: Hi, Ms. Cole. Are you doing anything?
Teacher: No. What do you want?
Student: I couldn't understand your lecture today.
Teacher: Well, I don't have time to explain now. Come back at 4:00.
Student: OK.
Teacher: Bye now.
Student: Bye-bye.

○ *Student:* _____
○ *Teacher:* _____
○ *Student:* _____
○ *Teacher:* _____
○ *Student:* _____
○ *Teacher:* _____
○ *Student:* _____
○

f Role-play these pairs of situations.

Student: You have an appointment to talk with your professor tomorrow afternoon, but you need to change the time.
Professor: Your schedule is very busy.

Student: You made plans to go to a movie with your friend at 10 p.m. tonight, but you're tired. You would like to go to an earlier movie.
Friend: You should finish studying before you go to the movie.

Student: You have three tests on the same day. You would like the professor to give his test on another day.
Professor: You can't change the day of the test.

Student: You have three tests on the same day. You promised your friend you would go out for dinner, but now you would like to do it on another day.
Friend: It's your birthday, and you really want to go out to celebrate.

▪ Lesson 5

The philosophy of right and wrong

a Rafael is reading an article as an assignment for his Business Ethics class. Read the article on page 11 and complete the notes.

> **extortion:** forcing someone to give you money by threatening them
> **poison:** something that will kill you if you eat it
> **reputation:** other people's opinion about you
> **crisis:** a serious and dangerous problem
> **recall:** to take a product back from stores to the factory

🍎 Warren's Food Products

The crisis:
Extortionists wanted (1) _____.
If they didn't get this, they would (2) _____ *in* (3) _____.
The company's response:
(1) *set up* _____
(2) *have a* _____
(3) _____ *tests*
(4) _____
Possible alternatives:
(1) _____
(2) _____
(3) _____
(4) *do nothing (police)*
What the company did:
(1) _____
(2) _____
(3) _____
Customers' reactions
(1) _____ (2) _____ (3) _____
The company's situation today:
_____

 b Look at the five alternatives discussed in the article. What are some possible results for each one? With a partner, discuss each alternative and list the results in your notebook.

c Discuss these questions with a group.

1. What are the responsibilities of a food company? Who are they responsible to?
2. Which alternative would be the best for the police? the extortionists? the customers? the factory workers? the company's profits?

Ethics and Extortion

by Carmen Cruz

Last year, Warren's Food Products, the country's largest producer of cookies, faced a crisis. Extortionists threatened to poison Warren's cookies in two major cities unless the company paid them $20 million. Warren's removed all its products from supermarkets in the two cities for two weeks, and this made the company lose millions of dollars. Managing Director Jessica Chang talked to *Business Today* about how her company handled the crisis.

According to Chang, dealing with the situation was simpler than it may seem. "You just give yourself some guiding lights—a bit like driving your car at night; if you've got lights, you've got no problem. We established our guiding lights on the first day, so it wasn't hard." The "lights" for Warren's consisted of principles. "First, we wanted to protect the safety of the public. Second, we wanted to protect the reputation of our company. Our customers have trusted us for 70 years. And third, we wanted to end the crisis as quickly as possible."

As soon as the company received the extortion message, they set up a crisis team of senior managers. The team met to assess the situation. "We had chemical tests of the poisoned cookies that the extortionist sent to us," says Chang. "The tests showed that one cookie would be enough to kill a two-year-old child. We had to react quickly."

The team had a heated discussion. Some members said that the company should only remove Fruit Dream cookies, since that was the poisoned brand that had been sent to Warren's. Others thought that all of the company's products should be recalled. "Some people felt we should take the cookies out all over the country," says Chang. She wanted to recall the company's products from the two cities named by the extortionists.

"The police didn't want us to take our products off the shelves. They were afraid that might encourage other extortionists," Chang reported. Experts said that in 48% of cases, extortionists give up without getting any money. There was a good chance that no one would actually be poisoned.

Warren's decided to remove the cookies. Within a few hours, they began taking back 300 products from over 30,000 stores in the two cities, and advertising on TV and radio about what they were doing. They set up a special telephone number that received 2,500 calls a day. Many customers supported the company. "People sent us letters and wrote poems. Children even sent us money."

But a year later, business is still not back to normal. Before the incident, Warren's sold 60% of the cookies in the country. Today, it's only 40%. As a result, two of the company's factories have closed, and hundreds of employees have been laid off. Still, Chang does not regret the company's decision. "In business, your reputation is your biggest asset. If you lose that, you can never get it back."

Lesson 6

If we go ahead with this plan . . .

a Rafael is talking to the international student advisor at his university. Read the conversation and complete the sentences using one of the phrases from the box.

I'll join the hiking club   my parents will be very upset
I'll get an A for the class   you won't enjoy your stay here
I'll talk to you again

Advisor: Come in, Rafael. Have a seat. How is everything going for you?

Rafael: Much better, thanks.

Advisor: What about your 20th Century Philosophy class?

Rafael: It's still hard, but my classmates and I formed a study group and that's helped me a lot. If I do well on the exam, (1) _____.

Advisor: That's good to hear! About how many hours a day do you study?

Rafael: Usually four or five hours in the evening . . . And all day Saturday and Sunday.

Advisor: You really should take a break more often. If you don't take time to relax, (2) _____.

Rafael: I'm sure you're right. If I have more time next semester, (3) _____.

Advisor: You don't have to wait until then!

Rafael: Well, I have to think about my family. If I don't get good grades, (4) _____.

Advisor: Your grades have improved a lot in the last few weeks. I've sure your parents are very proud of you.

Rafael: Thanks for all your help. If I have more problems, (5) _____.

b What will happen? Complete the sentences with your own ideas.

1. If our teacher gives us a lot of homework tonight, _____
   _____.

2. If I have time this weekend, _____
   _____.

3. If I get a good job after I graduate. _____
   _____.

4. If pollution in this country gets worse, _____
   _____.

5. If the government spends more for education, _____
   _____.

c Read this assignment from Rafael's Business Ethics class.

PHIL 420 Prof. Wolinsky
Week 3

Discussion assignment: Sweeten-Up

You and your group work for Beverex, a company that produces soft drinks. Beverex is about to launch a new product called Sweeten-Up, a kind of chocolate soda that will be marketed to children. The formula for this soda contains 50% more sugar than other drinks, because market research shows that children ages 5–12 prefer very sweet drinks and chocolate flavor. The advertising will feature Sweetie Bear, a cute cartoon bear that children like.

Beverex has not been very successful in the last few years. Sales are down, and many workers have lost their jobs. Old people are the main buyers of its other drinks, and they buy far fewer drinks than younger people. Other companies have produced drinks for teenagers, but they haven't yet marketed a special soda for children. If Sweeten-Up is successful, it will save your company.

There is one big problem. Lately, many people are criticizing soft drink companies. They say that eating and drinking too much sugar is harmful to children's health. In your country, over 70% of elementary school children have problems with their teeth, and 30% of children are overweight. People are concerned because this soda contains so much sugar.

The president of Beverex is very concerned. He has appointed a committee to talk about these questions:

1. Will this product harm children's health?
2. Should we change the advertising? If so, how?
3. Should we change the product? If so, how?
4. What effect would your suggestions have on children? employees? the company? the community?

Discuss these questions with your classmates.

d What will happen? Work with a partner to complete the sentences with your own ideas.

1. If children drink more soda, they will _____
_____.

2. If we go ahead with this plan, _____
_____.

3. If we don't sell more drinks,_____
_____.

4. If parents _____
_____.

5. If _____
_____.

6. If _____
_____.

e Get into a group and decide what Beverex should do and why. Have one student take notes of the group's ideas.

Task:

Carry out a survey on ethics

An international magazine is planning a special issue on "Right and Wrong." The editor has asked your team to write an article about some ethical questions in your country.

With your team:

1. Look back at the box on "Ethics in Daily Life" in Lesson 3. Together, write two more survey questions about situations in everyday life.

2. Carry out your survey. Each member of your team should interview as many classmates, friends, and family members as possible, in English or your own language, and write down all the answers.

3. Combine and organize all the answers that you received. Discuss what these answers mean with your group. Were there any differences in the answers of people of different ages?

4. Work together to write a short article explaining the results of your survey.

5. Read your article to the class.

Unit 2

Language

a Laura Castro will graduate from the university next month with a degree in Spanish and Portuguese. She also speaks English. What are some jobs that she could apply for? With a partner, list as many ideas as possible.

_____   _____   _____

_____   _____   _____

b Read this article and circle the careers that you didn't think of in Exercise **a**.

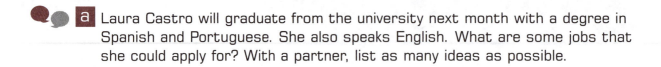

What can I do with a degree in foreign languages?

There are many types of job opportunities for majors in Languages and Literature. Some careers are directly related to speaking, reading, and writing proficiency in a particular language. These include teaching a foreign language and working in the mass media as a radio, TV, or newspaper journalist.

Many government agencies require language specialists such as translators and interpreters. International agencies such as NGOs (non-governmental organizations) also hire many graduates for their language skills. The United Nations and its branches are the world's largest employer of language specialists.

Proficiency in foreign languages also qualifies you for many jobs in business. For instance, you could work in tourism or the hotel industry, in financial or export companies, or in an advertising or public relations firm.

Finally, a degree from the Department of Languages and Literature gives excellent background training for advanced professional degrees in law, international banking and international business. And some graduates continue for advanced degrees in literature and become university professors.

c Review the job opportunities listed. Choose the three most interesting jobs and tell your partner why you chose them.

> *I want to work in . . . because . . .*

> *In my opinion, one of the most interesting jobs is . . .*

CD T-8 **d** Laura's classmate Jackie is helping her write her resume. Listen to their conversation and complete the resume.

Laura Castro
1267 Monroe Avenue
Anderson, CA 94590
Tel: (108) 555-3762
e-mail: lcastro@networld.com
Web site: www.networld.com/lcastro

Education:
Bachelor of Arts, Southland University, 2005
Major: (1) _____
Exchange student, University of Sao Paulo, Brazil, (2) _____

Work Experience:
Secretary, Latin American Cultural Society, summer 2003 and 2004
- (3) _____ in Spanish and Portuguese
- translated information on (4) _____
Office Assistant, Pacific Bank, summer 2002
- used word processing and spreadsheet software
- helped Spanish-speaking (5) _____
Volunteer, California Symphony Orchestra, 2002 - present
- interpreter for visiting international (6) _____
(7) _____:
- lived for (8) _____ years in Mexico
- traveled for one month in Brazil

e Write a similar resume for yourself.

f Exchange resumes with a partner and make suggestions for improvements. Use expressions like the ones below.

| (Maybe) You should . . .   If I were you, I would . . .   You could . . .   I (don't) think it's a good idea to . . . |

 g Now look at these job ads with a partner. Which would be the best for Laura? Why?

Language teachers for children

ABC Language Institute seeks enthusiastic, motivated part-time teachers of Spanish, French, and English. Work with children ages 4 - 10. Hours: 4 - 6 p.m. daily. Experience preferred. Apply online at . . .

International Sales

Major producer of office computer systems requires sales representative for Pacific region (East Asia and the Americas.) Requires college degree, knowledge of other languages. Send resume to . . .

TRANSLATOR

Join our team! Credit card company is looking for a Spanish-English translator for our new Latin America department. The ideal candidate has business experience and excellent communication skills. Please call . . .

■ Lesson 2
Can you tell me a little about yourself

a Laura is talking about the kind of job she wants. Look at the underlined verbs and write them in the correct section of the chart.

> *I enjoy working with words and ideas, but I really <u>dislike</u> doing the same thing every day . . . I <u>like</u> to have a lot of variety. <u>I'm good</u> at meeting deadlines. I <u>hate</u> to work in a noisy place, and I <u>hate</u> talking on the phone a lot. I <u>like</u> using my Spanish and Portuguese. I think I <u>want</u> to work in an international company. So I've <u>decided</u> to apply for a job at CreditPlus, a big credit card company. I <u>hope</u> to be a translator, and I <u>plan</u> to stay at my job for a long time . . .*

Verbs followed by infinitives	Verbs followed by gerunds	Verbs followed by gerunds or infinitives
decide	*enjoy*	*like*

b Write sentences about yourself in your notebook, using gerunds and infinitives.

1. I enjoy . . .	2. I hate . . .	3. I plan . . .
4. I am good at . . .	5. I want . . .	6. I like . . .

c Laura is getting ready for a job interview at CreditPlus. Read the article. With a partner, decide which advice is appropriate for your country too, and circle the numbers.

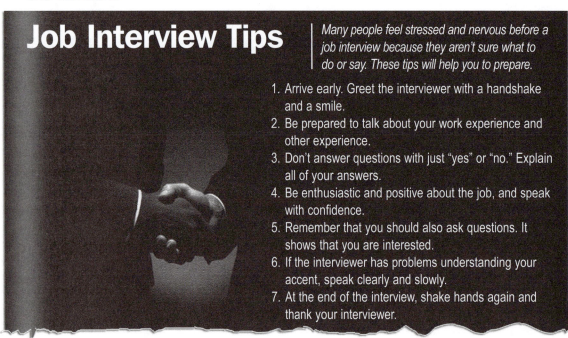

Job Interview Tips

Many people feel stressed and nervous before a job interview because they aren't sure what to do or say. These tips will help you to prepare.

1. Arrive early. Greet the interviewer with a handshake and a smile.
2. Be prepared to talk about your work experience and other experience.
3. Don't answer questions with just "yes" or "no." Explain all of your answers.
4. Be enthusiastic and positive about the job, and speak with confidence.
5. Remember that you should also ask questions. It shows that you are interested.
6. If the interviewer has problems understanding your accent, speak clearly and slowly.
7. At the end of the interview, shake hands again and thank your interviewer.

d With your partner, write three more tips for job interviews in your country.

1. _____

2. _____

3. _____

e Listen to Laura's interview and fill in the interviewer's questions.

CD
T-9

Interviewer: Good afternoon, Ms. Castro. I'm Rachel Carver, the Assistant Personnel Manager.

Laura: I'm pleased to meet you.

Interviewer: Now, first of all, (1) _____?

Laura: Well, I'm bilingual in English and Spanish. My father is Mexican and my mother is Canadian, and I grew up speaking both languages at home. My father's company transferred him to Mexico City when I was 14, so I went to high school there. Now I'm graduating with a degree in Spanish and Portuguese, and I really hope to use my knowledge of languages in my career.

Interviewer: That's a very interesting background. (2) _____
_____?

Laura: CreditPlus is one of the fastest-growing finance companies in North America, and the new Latin American branch is already very successful. I think your company has a very international perspective, and that's the kind of place that I would really like to work.

Interviewer: I'm glad to hear that. Now, (3) _____
_____?

Laura: Well, I can give you two reasons. One is my language skills. I speak two languages that will be very important in the future. The second reason is my international experience. I spent a year in Brazil as an exchange student, and lived for four years in Mexico with my family. So I'm familiar with the cultures and customs of those countries.

Interviewer: (4) _____?

Laura: Yes, I do. I translated brochures and advertising at the Latin American Cultural Society. I also translated e-mail messages for the director.

Interviewer: Your background is very impressive. You'll be hearing from us.

Laura: Thank you very much for meeting with me.

f Answer the questions with a partner.

1. Which of the tips in Exercise **c** did Laura follow? _____

2. Do you think the interview was successful? Why or why not? _____

_____

Lesson 3

Can you do a translation

a Laura got the job at CreditPlus. What advice would you give to a friend who is starting a new job?

1. _____
2. _____
3. _____
4. _____
5. _____

b It's Laura's first day at work, and she gets a telephone call. Number the lines to put them in the correct order.

___ **Laura:** Of course. What can I do for you?

_1_ **Laura:** Good morning, this is Corporate Communications.

___ **Alex:** May I speak with Laura Castro?

___ **Alex:** This is Alex Chung in the Marketing Department. We have a translation project for you. Do you have a few minutes to discuss it with me?

___ **Laura:** I can take care of that. And what's the deadline?

___ **Alex:** We have a new web page about our credit cards. We need it translated into Spanish for customers in South America.

___ **Laura:** Speaking.

___ **Laura:** I'll have it ready for you by 1:00.

___ **Alex:** Great! Then I'll send it to you by e-mail.

___ **Alex:** I'm afraid we need it for a meeting at 2 p.m. tomorrow.

c Look at the conversation and find the polite expressions that have these meanings.

1. Hi. _____
2. Is Laura there? _____
3. Can you talk to me now? _____
4. What do you want? _____
5. OK. _____
6. I can do that. _____

d Write these polite expressions for business telephone conversations in the correct space.

> Could you spell that, please?
> Sorry, I didn't hear that.
> Could I have the ___ department, please?
> I'd like to speak to ___, please.
> Could I leave a message?
>
> Please tell him / her . . .
> Hello, this is ___ from ___.
> My name is ___, calling from ___.
> Is ___ there, please?
> Excuse me, I didn't catch your name.

Introducing yourself	**Asking for someone**
Leaving a message	**Asking for repetition**

e Look at these situations and circle *Formal* or *Informal*. Then role-play the phone calls with a partner.

1. You call your co-worker to ask him / her to check your English in a business letter you've written.	Formal	Informal
2. You call your boss to explain that you need more information before you can translate the advertisement.	Formal	Informal
3. You call your friend to say you can't meet him / her tonight at 7:00. You have to work late.	Formal	Informal
4. You call your teacher to say that you are going to be absent from class for a week because of an illness in your family.	Formal	Informal

f Read the tips and check ✔ the ones that are the same in your country. Compare your answers with a partner's.

> **Telephone Etiquette in English**
> ···
>
> ___ When you call someone, identify yourself after the person says hello.
> ___ Ask if the person has time to talk to you before you start the conversation.
> ___ Explain the reason for your call.
> ___ Speak clearly, and avoid eating or chewing gum while on the phone.
> ___ Repeat important information you've heard to check that you've understood it.
> ___ When you leave a message on voice mail or an answering machine, include your name, phone number, and reason for calling.

g Write a short paragraph explaining the rules of telephone etiquette to foreigners who are visiting your country.

■ **Lesson 4**

Linking languages

a Where is it spoken? Match the language with the country

1. Swahili ___   a. Brazil
2. Farsi ___   b. Philippines
3. Urdu ___   c. Iran
4. Arabic ___   d. Egypt
5. Philipino ___   e. India
6. Portuguese ___   f. Pakistan
7. French ___   g. Kenya
8. Hindi ___   h. Canada

b Read the article on page 23. Then answer the questions with a partner.

1. What is the difference between a translator and an interpreter?
2. What happens when a customer calls Interlink?

c Find this information in the article.

1. how many new employees Interlink will have this year _____
2. the number of languages Interlink works with _____
3. how many calls an interpreter of an African language gets per week _____
4. the location of Interlink's offices _____
5. the number of people in the U.S. who don't speak English well _____
6. the number of calls Interlink can receive in one second _____
7. two kinds of businesses that use Interlink _____

d Match these words from the article with their meanings.

1. proficient ___   a. pronunciation that shows what country you're from
2. mother tongue ___   b. popular informal words
3. dialect ___   c. technical words used in one subject
4. accent ___   d. first language
5. slang ___   e. form of a language spoken in only one place
6. terminology ___   f. able to do something well

e Discuss these questions.

1. If a tourist in your country has language problems, how can he or she get help?
2. What are some possible problems with telephone interpreting?
3. Would you like to work as a telephone interpreter? Explain your reasons.
4. Can computers translate languages as well as people can? Why or why not?

Linking Languages

In an office in Los Angeles, a woman answers the phone. "What language can I help you with today?" she asks the caller. She listens for a moment, then types a few numbers into a computer. A minute later, a Japanese-language interpreter is helping the caller communicate with his English-speaking doctor — by telephone.

In the United States, an estimated 7 million people speak little or no English. Interlink is the country's largest provider of telephone interpretation. It works with over 150 different languages. For some languages, such as Chinese, there are even interpreters of different **dialects**. Many of their customers are individuals, like the Japanese man visiting his doctor. Others are government agencies, or large corporations such as insurance and credit card companies.

Interlink was founded ten years ago by Randall Petri, a former international banker. It now has 170 full-time employees and 2,500 interpreters. All customers' calls go to the company's main office in Los Angeles, and a computer sends the calls to interpreters around the world. Interpreters of the most common languages (including Spanish, Korean, and Russian) work at the company's two offices, in the U.S. and Peru. The others work at home.

"All of our interpreters work in their **mother tongue**, and we give them a test to make sure they are **proficient** in English too," says Petri. "We also check to make sure that their **accent** is easy to understand, and that they know current **slang** expressions."

About 70% of Interlink calls are in Spanish, and most calls are about simple, everyday matters. A Vietnamese man has a problem with his credit card company, or a woman from Colombia wants a telephone in her new apartment. But some calls are true emergencies. "We work with police departments in many cities," says Petri. "And some of the calls are very stressful. For example, a woman called one night from her bedroom and said a burglar was walking around in her house."

Sometimes there are cultural problems, too. "We had a call from a Korean man. His wife was having trouble breathing. But he wanted to do the correct formal introduction with our interpreter, saying, 'My name is Mr. Kim, this is the name of my village in Korea.' And he wanted to know about the interpreter too!" The interpreter called an ambulance, and the caller's wife recovered in the hospital.

Some interpreters specialize in medical or legal **terminology**, or uncommon languages. "Someone who speaks an African language may get only one call a week," said Petri. "We pay them to stay home and wait for calls. If they receive a call, they are also paid per minute."

Petri pointed to a computer that shows which interpreters are logged on. Speakers of Urdu, Italian, Russian, and Farsi were all at work. "Now there are 34 Spanish interpreters logged on, but that could change in a minute. For example, if the electricity goes off in Texas, we might get 1000 calls in a second. Then we'll go to our interpreters in New York and Puerto Rico." Business is growing every day, and Petri expects to hire 200 more part-time interpreters this year.

Lesson 5
We need the translation tomorrow

 a Do this experiment, in groups with three, five, or seven members.

1. The first student writes a long sentence (at least ten words) in English at the top of a sheet of paper.

2. The next student reads the sentence, folds the paper over, and writes a translation at the top of the paper.

3. The next student reads the translated sentence, folds the paper over, and translates it back into English.
   Continue until everyone in the group has translated the sentence.

4. Look at the first and last versions of the sentence together, and talk about what happened.

CD T-10 **b** Laura comes back to her office after a meeting and finds three messages in her voice mail. Listen to the messages and complete the forms. One piece of information is missing on each form.

Project 1

Translation request
Person requesting: _____ Department: _____
Type of project: _____
Subject: _____
Readers: _____
Deadline: _____
Size of project: _____

Project 2

Translation request
Person requesting: _____ Department: _____
Type of project: _____
Subject: _____
Readers: _____
Deadline: _____
Size of project: _____

Project 3

Translation request
Person requesting: _____ Department: _____
Type of project: _____
Subject: _____
Readers: _____
Deadline: _____
Size of project: _____

c Which project will be the most difficult? Which project should she do first?

d Laura's friend Jackie is working for a movie company, writing English subtitles for Spanish language movies. She's telling Laura about her problems at work. Read the sentences and check ✔ the correct answers.

1. "If my boss gave me the movies earlier, I would have more time to write the subtitles."
   She has a lot of time to work.   yes ☐   no ☐
2. "If I had more time for each for each movie, I could do really good subtitles."
   She thinks her subtitles aren't very good.   yes ☐   no ☐
3. "If I weren't so busy, I could have lunch with my coworkers and get to know them."
   She eats together with her coworkers.   yes ☐   no ☐
4. "If I don't finish my work by 6:00, I have to stay late, or come in early the next day."
   She sometimes goes home after 6:00.   yes ☐   no ☐
5. "If I stay late at work, I miss dinner with my family."
   She always eats dinner at home.   yes ☐   no ☐
6. "If I didn't feel so stressed, it would be fun working with movies."
   She enjoys her job now.   yes ☐   no ☐

e What advice and suggestions can you give Jackie? Role-play a conversation between Laura and Jackie.

f Write unreal conditional sentences about what you would do in these situations.

1. (have a lot of free time) _____

   _____
2. (win the lottery) _____

   _____
3. (teach this class) _____

   _____
4. (be president of this country) _____

   _____
5. (can travel anywhere in the world) _____

   _____

g Discuss these situations.

1. Imagine that you could have any job in the world. Which job would you choose? Why?
2. Imagine that you could have dinner with any famous person who is alive today. Who would you choose? Why?
3. Imagine that you could live in any year in the past. Which year would you choose? Why?

Lesson 6

A report on our services

a Laura's boss has asked her to write a report on the company's services for Spanish-speaking customers. Read her report and fill in the headings.

Introduction	Customer Service
Advertising	Online Information
Recommendations	

A report gives the important facts on a topic written in an impersonal style. It is usually divided into sections with separate headings. Often, it makes recommendations.

(1) *Introduction*

This report discusses our company's services for our Spanish-speaking customers. In the past three years, their number has increased by 70%. We now have customers in twelve Latin American countries, from Mexico to Chile.

(2) _____

The company's Web site currently has a few new pages in Spanish. There is information about our credit cards, and articles about financial topics. Many customers don't realize that there is a Web site in Spanish.

(3) _____

Last year, the customer service department hired ten new representatives who speak Spanish. This has been very successful, and they now receive almost 200 calls in Spanish every day. This service is available from 9 a.m. to 5 p.m. However, after 5 p.m., there is service only in English.

(4) _____

The company now has newspaper and magazine advertisements in Spanish in four countries in Latin America. The ads are translations of our ads in the United States, and they have not been very successful. People say they don't have confidence in a foreign company.

(5) _____

The company should make more efforts to serve its Spanish-speaking customers. We need special advertising that is designed to fit the culture of each country. These ads should tell readers to visit our Spanish Web site. We also need to hire more customer service representatives to answer calls in Spanish. If possible, the service hours should be extended until at least 10 p.m. By doing these things, we will increase our business in the growing Latin American market.

b What would happen if the situation were different? Write sentences.

1. Customers don't know about the Spanish Web site.
   If _____.

2. The Web site has only a few pages in Spanish.
   If _____.

3. The company doesn't have very good ads in Spanish.
   If _____.

4. Customer Service isn't available in Spanish in the evening.
   If _____.

c Write your own report on this topic: *Opportunities for students in my country to practice their English.* Divide your report into sections and give each one a heading. Your report should answer these questions. Make notes for each section before you write.

1. Do students have enough opportunities to practice their English?

   _____

2. How can they practice listening and speaking?

   _____

3. How can they practice reading and writing?

   _____

4. What recommendations do you have?

   _____

 d Exchange papers with a partner, and comment on your partner's paper. Then discuss your recommendations. What would happen?

e Circle your answers on this survey.

OPINION POLL: Language

Do you agree or disagree with these statements?

1. English will be more important in my country in the future.

| Agree strongly | Agree somewhat | Disagree somewhat | Disagree strongly |

2. All children in the world should learn a second language.

| Agree strongly | Agree somewhat | Disagree somewhat | Disagree strongly |

3. You can't really understand a country if you don't speak its language.

| Agree strongly | Agree somewhat | Disagree somewhat | Disagree strongly |

4. Nowadays people use too many English words in my language.

| Agree strongly | Agree somewhat | Disagree somewhat | Disagree strongly |

5. There are some words that you can't really translate into another language.

| Agree strongly | Agree somewhat | Disagree somewhat | Disagree strongly |

---

f Compare your answers with your classmate's. Explain your reasons.

Team Project 2

Task:
Plan a Web site

An international organization called Students Helping Students has asked your team to prepare a Web site on how to be a successful language learner. Students in different countries will use the Web site to get ideas for learning English.

With your team:

1. Give your Web site a name.
2. Draw plans on paper for each Web page. You should include a home page, which introduces your Web site and gives general information about learning English. Make separate Web pages for different areas such as pronunciation, listening, or idioms. Each team member should plan a page for a different area, with useful tips for students.
3. Make your Web pages lively and interesting with graphics and illustrations such as drawings or photos.
4. Post your plans on the classroom wall for your classmates to read.
5. Decide which Web page provides the most useful information.

Unit 3

Art

We help artists sell their work

a Listen to the radio interview and complete the profile.

CD
T-11

Name: Jason Lee
Nationality: (1) _____ Job: (2) _____
(3) _____ : Arts Unlimited
Purposes of organization:
● give advice to (4) _____ ● develop programs for
(5) _____
Countries he's worked in: (6) _____, _____
Example of program: (7) _____ for people who make traditional crafts
Purpose of his visit:
● (8) _____ with artists and craftspeople
● plan a national program to (9) _____
His art form: (10) _____
Specialty: (11) _____, especially _____ and _____

b Read the article. Then answer the questions with a partner.

☞ Art or Craft? ☜

Today, there is a lot of discussion about the meaning of the words *art* and *craft*. Both are ways that people create new things. So, what is the difference between them?

Basically, *art* expresses human ideas and experiences through painting, drawing, sculpture, etc. Most artists take formal classes for many years at art academies. Every piece they make is completely different. Their work is sold for high prices, and can be seen in galleries and museums.

A *craft* is a way of making beautiful objects by hand, often in a traditional way. Each country and culture has its own unique crafts, such as weaving, woodworking, and pottery. People generally learn to do a craft by working individually with an experienced craftsperson, or they may learn it from older members of their family.

Sometimes it's difficult to say what is an art, or what is a craft. If someone paints a mural of animals on the side of a building, is that art? If someone makes a bowl so beautiful that it is put in a museum, is that a craft? Questions like these are hard to answer, but both artists and craftspeople bring joy and beauty to the world.

1. Who are some of the most famous artists in your country today? _____
_____

2. What traditional crafts are still made in your country? Which parts of the country do they come from?
_____

3. In your city, where can you go to see fine art? _____
_____

4. Is there a place to buy traditional crafts in your city? _____
_____

5. In your country, is it easy for an artist or craftsperson to make a living? Why or why not?
_____

c Write the words below in the correct column. Some can be used more than once. Then add your own.

jewelry	bowl	picture	cup	box	rug	scarf	chair
	vase	bag	mural	sculpture			

1. ceramics   _____   _____   _____   _____
2. woodworking   _____   _____   _____   _____
3. weaving   _____   _____   _____   _____
4. metalworking   _____   _____   _____   _____
5. painting   _____   _____   _____   _____

d The Minister of Culture is telling Jason about problems artists have had. Look at the underlined verbs and answer the questions.

> *"We wanted to build a craft museum in 2004, but we didn't have enough money.*
> *If we <u>had had</u> enough money in 2004, we <u>would have built</u> a craft museum."*
> *"The weather was bad last year, so we didn't get many tourists.*
> *If the weather <u>had been</u> better, we <u>would have gotten</u> many tourists."*

1. Do the sentences talk about the past or the present? _____
2. Is the situation real or not real? _____

e Write similar conditional sentences about these situations.

1. The country didn't have many tourists, so hotels and stores lost money.

_____

2. People didn't know about the art show, so they didn't visit the museum.

_____

3. We started craft programs in school, so crafts became very popular.

_____

4. Visitors had very little information about the crafts, so they didn't buy them.

_____

f When the government helps artists, what effect does that have on the country and its economy?

Lesson 2

Getting the facts

a Jason attends a meeting at the Ministry of Culture, where he has a briefing about Zimbaco. Listen and fill in the blanks.

CD
T-12

The Republic of Zimbaco is one of the world's newest nations. It became independent in (1) _____ , but it has a long history. People have been living on this beautiful island for more than (2) _____ years. Today, the population is around (3) _____ people, and it is growing rapidly. Because we have very limited land for farming and little industry, we have to import many products from other countries. The cost of living is very high. Because of this, many traditional craftspeople have gotten jobs and have stopped producing crafts.

Zimbaco is divided into (4) _____ provinces. Our capital, Zimbaco City, is located in the Northern Province on the coast and has a population of (5) _____ people. The climate here is tropical, and many tourists come for vacations at one of our (6) _____ beach resorts. Unfortunately, very few visitors go into the city to buy crafts. They spend most of their time at the beach. The most famous craft in this region is woodcarvings from tropical trees.

The Eastern and Southern provinces have a mild climate that is good for farming. The people like to decorate the outside of their houses with beautiful wall paintings. Now a group of about (7) _____ craftspeople have begun selling boxes, dolls, and picture frames decorated with this traditional painting. This area is also famous for its traditional food, especially fruit and meat. These products must be refrigerated, though, so tourists don't like to buy them.

The Western Province is cut off by mountains. There are (8) _____ small cities, but they can only be visited by boat. People in the region earn a living from fishing, and they also make beautiful crafts from shells.

The Central Province is (9) _____ percent desert, with only about (10) _____ people living in small villages. The desert people are famous for their beautiful pottery and weavings, which they have produced for centuries. However, the roads are poor and there are few facilities for tourists. Because of this, it's very difficult for craftspeople to earn a living there, and many of them are moving to the cities to get jobs.

b What are some problems that the country has in selling its arts and crafts to tourists?

1. *Many traditional craftspeople have gotten jobs and have stopped producing crafts.*
2. _____
3. _____
4. _____
5. _____

c After the meeting, staff from the Ministry of Culture take Jason to see how some traditional crafts are made. Complete his notes, using passive sentences like the example.

Traditional craft A

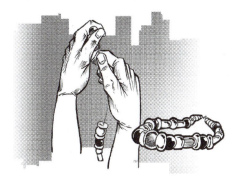

1. first / a long piece of glass / heat in the flame
First, a long piece of glass is heated in the flame.

2. next / the soft glass / shape into a bead

_____

3. after that / the beads / cool slowly

_____

4. finally / they / make into a necklace

_____

Traditional craft B

1. first / flour, sugar, and spices / mix in a large bowl

_____

2. then / an egg / add

_____

3. next / the dough / make into different shapes

_____

4. after that / the cookies / bake for an hour

_____

5. finally / they / pack in boxes

_____

d Complete these sentences with the correct form of the verb, active or passive.

1. Every year, thousands of tourists _____ (visit) Zimbaco.
2. English _____ (speak) as a second language in the country.
3. Wood _____ (use) in many traditional crafts there.
4. Beautiful vases and cups _____ (make) by people in the desert.
5. Zimbaco's Independence Day _____ (celebrate) on October 15.
6. Farmers in the Eastern Province _____ (grow) many kinds of fruit.
7. Crafts _____ (sell) in small shops across the country.
8. Tourists _____ (love) the warm climate and beautiful beaches.

 e Write a paragraph to explain how a special product in your country is made or cooked. Use passive sentences.

f Exchange paragraphs with a partner and make suggestions for improvement.

Lesson 3

I'm not so sure about that

a Jason is at a meeting with Zimbacan artists. Read their discussion in groups of three. Then find the expressions to complete the chart.

George: In my opinion, the problem for artists in Zimbaco is that nobody knows about our art and crafts.

Mona: I agree with you. If tourists don't know about our work, they won't buy it. We need lots of international TV ads.

Stella: I'm not so sure about that. TV ads are very expensive, and we don't know if they're effective. I think we need to make more places to sell crafts — places that are more convenient for tourists.

George: You're probably right . . . Most artists live in small towns. Tourists don't go there.

Stella: That's exactly what I think. We really need a large shopping center in Zimbaco City just for crafts. It could have a store for pottery, a store for wood carvings, and so on. We could put it near the airport.

Mona: But we already have a National Crafts Center. We just need advertising to tell people about it.

Stella: It's much too small. I think we need a bigger one.

George: Actually, I think a Web site is a better way to promote our crafts. With a Web site, we could sell them directly to customers all around the world.

Stella: I hate to disagree with you, but people need to see and touch the crafts in a store.

George: Oh, I don't think so. Online shopping is getting more popular in a lot of countries.

Expressions for agreeing	Expressions for disagreeing
_____	_____
_____	_____
_____	_____

b What is each person's plan?

1. George _____
2. Mona _____
3. Stella _____

c Think of three other ideas to help the craftspeople of Zimbaco sell more of their work. Then work with a partner to take turns presenting your ideas and agreeing or disagreeing with what you hear.

> *I think the government should pay all artists a salary.*
>
> *I'm not so sure about that. If the government does that . . .*

d Look at the adjectives from the conversation and complete the chart.

Adjective	Comparative form
1. expensive	
2. effective	
3.	more convenient
4. small	
5. large	
6.	bigger
7.	better
8.	more popular

e Write ads for these Zimbaco crafts comparing them with factory-made products. Use the adjectives given.

Handmade Zimbaco
vase

beautiful	large	strong
heavy	decorative	expensive

1. *This handmade Zimbaco vase is much more beautiful than the factory-made vase.*
It _____
_____
_____
_____
_____
_____
_____

Factory-made
vase

pretty	traditional	big
colorful	warm	elegant

2. _____
_____
_____
_____
_____
_____
_____
_____
_____

Factory-made
shawl

Handmade Zimbaco
shawl

 f Imagine that a foreign artist has come to your school to give a presentation. Your teacher has asked your group to choose a gift for the guest. The gift should be something handmade in your country or your city. The present will be bought by the members of your class, so it shouldn't be too expensive. Work together to decide on a gift, using the polite expressions for agreeing and disagreeing.

g Explain your group's decision to the class. Then vote for the best idea in the class.

Lesson 4
Keeping traditional arts alive

a Jason has prepared a report about some successful art programs in other countries. Read the report on page 37 and complete the chart.

Name of program:			
Year started:			
Country or countries:			
Kind of program:	Web site	craft trails	
How it works:			
Where people buy the crafts:			in a traditional market
Examples of crafts:			

b Write sentences comparing the programs using the adjectives below. Explain your reasons.

1. easy to start (museum, Web site) _A Web site is easier to start than a museum because you don't need much money._

2. practical (Web site, craft trails) _____

_____

3. enjoyable (craft trails, museum) _____

_____

4. useful for artists (craft trails, museum) _____

_____

5. good for tourism (museum, Web site) _____

_____

 **c** Discuss these questions in groups.

1. If you want to buy an unusual and special present for someone, where do you go shopping?
2. Where are some interesting or unusual places to go shopping in your city? How often do you go there?

Keeping Traditional Arts Alive

Kentucky is a state in the southeastern part of the United States. The Appalachian Mountains run through Kentucky, and because the landscape is very rugged, transportation is difficult and the economy is undeveloped. Many of Kentucky's traditional crafts are still made in tiny mountain towns, and they include candles, baskets, quilts, and handmade wooden furniture. Hundreds of craftspeople work in the area. But these artists live far from the cities, and it can be very difficult for tourists to find their studios.

To help these artists, the state government started a program called the Kentucky Artisan Heritage Trails in 2001. First, they planned twelve different driving tours to different parts of the mountains. Then they printed maps and driving directions for all of the tours. Tourists drive along the Trails through beautiful mountain scenery and stop at different artists' studios. There, they can watch the artists at work and buy crafts directly from them. Visitors enjoy meeting and talking with the artists, and the artists get a better price for their work.

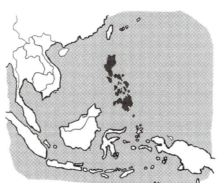

Many people call the Korean Folk Village near Seoul a "living museum." When the Folk Village was built in 1974, more than 200 old buildings from all around South Korea were brought there. At the outdoor museum, visitors can walk through farmhouses, city homes, a Buddhist temple, and even a traditional school. But unlike in other museums, dozens of people live here and work in traditional ways.

Inside an old farmhouse, a woman weaves cloth for a coat. In another building, an elderly man in a big black hat does traditional ink painting on a long piece of paper. You can watch artists make pots, bamboo baskets, paper, and even traditional rice candy. Best of all, you can buy all of the things they make in a traditional market in the Folk Village. And when you're finished shopping, there is a place to relax and try old-fashioned Korean food—in traditional outdoor restaurants.

In 1979, an Englishman named Roy Scott was working for the United Nations in the Philippines. He met a group of craftspeople who produced hand-made baskets to sell in stores overseas. Unfortunately the stores had found cheaper baskets from other countries. In order to help these craftspeople, Scott began sending their baskets directly to the UK. The baskets quickly became very popular.

This was the origin of One Village, an organization that sells handmade products from India, Bangladesh, and Nepal, as well as the Philippines. Through their Web site, OneVillage.com, customers can shop online for beautiful rugs, curtains, lamps, baskets, and other items for the home. All of these crafts are made by cooperative groups of artists in developing countries, and One Village pays them a good price for all of their products. The goal of One Village is to build up communities by supporting traditional arts and crafts.

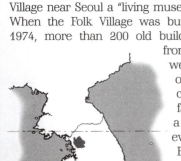

Lesson 5

Our objective in this meeting . . .

a Jason is attending a meeting at the Ministry of Culture. Listen to the introduction and complete Jason's notes about the first part of the meeting.

CD T-13

Meeting: 2/24/06   Ministry of Culture

Reason for meeting: (1) _____

Government will spend (2) $ _____

New program to: (3) _____

Have proposals for: (4) _____ programs

Have chosen: (5) _____ proposals

Today's objective: (6) _____

b Role-play the meeting with two other students. Agree and disagree politely, and give reasons to support your plan. With your group, decide which plan to carry out next year.

Student A:
You are the Director of the National Museum. You want to start a new outdoor museum called the Zimbaco Traditional Village near Zimbaco City. It will have workshops for artists and craftspeople.

Student B:
You are the Minister of Tourism. You want to develop a program of driving trips to craft studios called the Zimbaco Heritage Tours. It will have maps and signs to show the way to art and craft studios.

Student C:
You are the Minister of Economic Development. You want to set up a Web site called ZimbaCraft.com to promote and sell crafts from Zimbaco around the world.

c With your group, design an advertisement for the program that you've chosen.

d Take turns showing your ads to the class and explaining your reasons for choosing the program. Which idea is the most popular? the cheapest? the most expensive?

e With a partner, take this art quiz.

1. The largest art museum in the world, with 24 km of galleries, is . . .
   - a. the Louvre, in Paris.
   - b. the Metropolitan Museum, in New York.
   - c. the Hermitage, in St. Petersburg.
2. The most active artist ever, who painted 13,500 paintings, was . . .
   - a. Picasso.
   - b. Da Vinci.
   - c. Van Gogh.
3. The oldest painting in the world, on the wall of a cave, is in . . .
   - a. Nigeria.
   - b. Peru.
   - c. France.
4. The costliest painting in the world, the Mona Lisa, was insured for . . .
   - a. $83 million.
   - b. $100 million.
   - c. $117 million.
5. The most expensive drawing in the world, which sold for $8.6 million, was made by . . .
   - a. Michelangelo.
   - b. Van Gogh.
   - c. Rembrandt.

f Fill in the superlative forms of these adjectives in the correct column.

busy	rich	noisy
difficult	attractive	talented
fine	interesting	small
easy	young	heavy

oldest	*costliest*	*most active*

g Write sentences with superlatives. Give your own opinions.

1. exciting / sport / the world _____ *Soccer is the most exciting sport in the world.*
2. famous / author / my country _____
3. great / painter / in history _____
4. interesting / book / that I've read _____
5. beautiful / place / my country _____
6. funny / movie / that I've seen _____
7. good / singer / the world _____

h Read this brochure and fill in the correct form of the adjective—*comparative* or *superlative*.

Zimbaco City Shopping Guide: Crafts

	Seaside Gallery	Emma's Crafts	Traditional Treasures
Quality of crafts	☆	☆☆☆	☆☆☆☆☆
Service	☺☺☺☺	☺☺	☺
Location	👍👍👍👍	👍👍👍	👍
Prices	$$$	$	$$$$$

Zimbaco City has only three craft shops, but they are quite different. Traditional Treasures sells (1) _____ (high) quality of crafts, including weavings, pottery, jewelry, and even traditional food products. However, it's also (2) _____ (expensive) shop. The products at Emma's Crafts are (3) _____ (cheap) than at Traditional Treasures, and the service is (4) _____ (friendly). Here, you'll find many crafts from the Northern and Central Provinces. It also has (5) _____ (low) prices in Zimbaco City. Seaside Gallery is even (6) _____ (friendly) than Emma's Crafts, and it has (7) _____ (beautiful) location of these shops. It's directly on the beach. There's only one problem. It sells (8) _____ (ugly) crafts in Zimbaco!

Lesson 6

What should we do to help . . .

 Read these letters in the *Zimbaco Daily Times* and underline the topic sentences. Then note the supporting details.

> ✓ *A good paragraph has a topic sentence that states the main idea and supporting details that explain the main idea.*

Zimbaco Daily Times

Reader Forum

We asked our readers: "What should we do to help our country's artists?"

A I believe that Zimbaco needs a national program of awards for its artists. We could give prizes of money every year to the best woodworkers, weavers, and all of our other traditional craftspeople. This would encourage artists to do their best work. It would also give fame and recognition to artists in very small towns. And finally, the money would be very helpful to artists with small incomes. I hope the government will consider this idea. — *Solomon H.*

B Too many of our old customs in Zimbaco have been forgotten. The government should start a national school for traditional arts and crafts. Today, there is no place where young people can go to study these arts, so many of them are dying out. A school would also promote higher quality work in the arts. And it would help to develop new techniques and products for the future. For all of these reasons, I think this academy would be very valuable for our country. — *Rebekah O.*

C The best way to support our artists is to buy their work! You can give traditional crafts for holiday and birthday presents, instead of machine-made junk. To decorate your home, office, or classroom, buy a painting or photograph from a local artist, instead of a poster from a factory. And for holidays and special occasions, wear our beautiful traditional handmade clothes, instead of an imported outfit. If we all do these things, our craftspeople will have a good life. — *Naomi T.*

Letter A
1. *would encourage artists to do their best work*
2. _____
_____
3. _____
_____

Letter B
1. _____
_____
2. _____
_____
3. _____
_____

Letter C
1. _____
_____
2. _____
_____
3. _____
_____

🖋 **b** Choose one of the arts below. Write a paragraph about the best way for your country to support this art. Include a topic sentence that contains your main idea, and give at least three reasons as supporting details.

| architecture | music | photography | theater | painting | literature |

c Work with a partner who wrote about a different art form. Exchange paragraphs and make suggestions for improvements.

d Read the ad. Then imagine that you are a member of the nominating committee for these awards. In groups, nominate two people for each of these awards and make notes for your reasons.

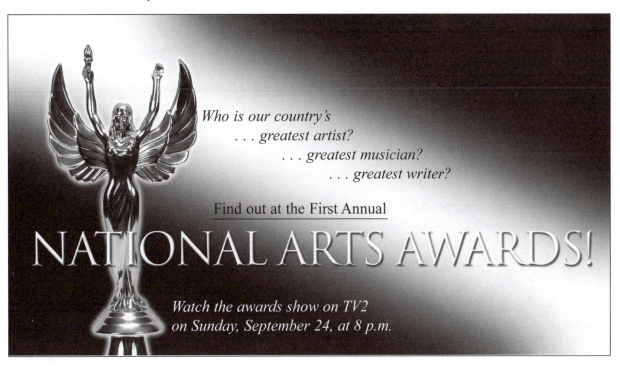

Who is our country's
...greatest artist?
...greatest musician?
...greatest writer?

Find out at the First Annual

NATIONAL ARTS AWARDS!

Watch the awards show on TV2
on Sunday, September 24, at 8 p.m.

1. greatest artist _____

   _____

2. greatest musician _____

   _____

3. greatest writer _____

   _____

e Take turns announcing your nominees to the class, and explaining the reasons why they were chosen. With the class, vote on a winner for each award.

Task:
Give a presentation on your country's arts

The Ministry of Tourism has asked your team to prepare a presentation on a unique art form from your country. This presentation will be given at international tourism shows in foreign countries.

1. With your team, choose a kind of art form, such as:
   - a type of music
   - a type of dance
   - a traditional craft
   - a kind of theater performance
   - a traditional food
   - a traditional way of making buildings

2. On a large sheet of paper, draw a poster about the art you've chosen, using words and drawings to answer these questions:
   - What is unique and special about this art?
   - How is it made, done, or performed?
   - Who are the artists, performers, or craftsmen?
   - Where can visitors see, buy, or experience this art?

Prepare to explain this information to the class.

3. Give your presentation in front of the class, using your poster to illustrate your talk. Each member of the team should give one part of the presentation.

Unit 4

History

Preserving the past

a Read the Web site about the organization and mark the statements *T* for *True* or *F* for *False*. Change the *false* statements to make them *true*.

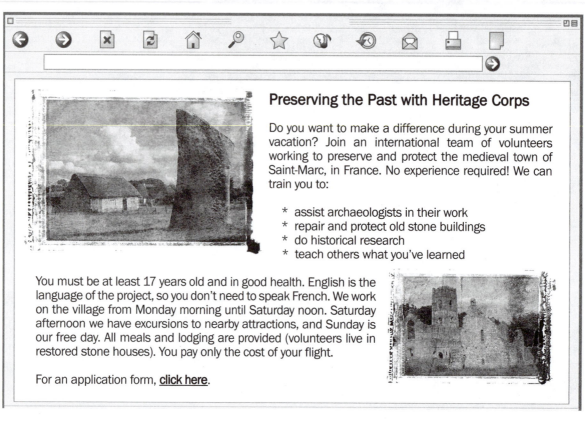

Preserving the Past with Heritage Corps

Do you want to make a difference during your summer vacation? Join an international team of volunteers working to preserve and protect the medieval town of Saint-Marc, in France. No experience required! We can train you to:

* assist archaeologists in their work
* repair and protect old stone buildings
* do historical research
* teach others what you've learned

You must be at least 17 years old and in good health. English is the language of the project, so you don't need to speak French. We work on the village from Monday morning until Saturday noon. Saturday afternoon we have excursions to nearby attractions, and Sunday is our free day. All meals and lodging are provided (volunteers live in restored stone houses). You pay only the cost of your flight.

For an application form, <u>click here</u>.

1. You must speak French to work on this project.	T	F
2. The volunteers work in an old village.	T	F
3. Heritage Corps pays for your plane ticket to France.	T	F
4. Volunteers come from several different countries.	T	F
5. You need experience to work on this project.	T	F
6. Some teenagers can work with Heritage Corps.	T	F

 b Discuss the questions in groups.

1. Why do people do volunteer work?
2. What are some well-known organizations that use volunteers?
3. What kinds of volunteer projects are there in your city? Your country?
4. Talk about experiences you or a friend has had doing volunteer work.

c Read the application form for new volunteers at Heritage Corps on page 45. Discuss the meaning of the words below with your partner.

1. age
2. gender
3. marital status
4. employer
5. citizenship
6. zip code
7. date of birth
8. educational institution
9. major
10. degree

d Complete the application with information about yourself.

Heritage Corps Volunteer Application

Name: _____
       Last   First   Middle

Mailing address: _____
City / State: _____ Zip code: _____ Country: _____
Phone: _____ E-mail address: _____
Gender: _____ Date of birth: _____ Citizenship: _____
Marital status: _____
Name of parent or guardian (if under 18): _____

List all educational institutions attended, beginning with most recent:

Institution	City	Dates	Degree/major
_____	_____	_____	_____
_____	_____	_____	_____
_____	_____	_____	_____

List jobs held, beginning with most recent:

Employer	Position	Dates	Responsibilities
_____	_____	_____	_____

List your hobbies, interests, and activities:
_____

I certify that all information in this application is accurate and complete to the best of my knowledge.
Signature _____ Date _____
Signature of parent or guardian (if under 18) _____

---

e Emilie Duval is a volunteer for Heritage Corps. Listen to her introduce herself, and complete the profile.

Name: Emilie Duval
Position: (1) _____
Hometown: Toulouse, in the (2) _____
of (3) _____
Student at (4) _____
Major: (5) _____
Special interest: Medieval period, years (6) _____
to _____
Work with Heritage Corps:
(7) 1. _____ archaeologists-made lists
(8) 2. helped to rebuild Le Blanc _____ with stone
(9) 3. this year: _____

■ Lesson 2

Life wasn't easy

a The new volunteers are having an orientation day. Read this quiz and work with a partner to guess the answers.

Life in Medieval Europe wasn't easy!
How hard was it?
Guess the answers.

1. People took a bath once a ___.
       a. day   b. week   c. month

2. The main food for ordinary people was ___.
       a. meat   b. rice   c. bread

3. The average person died at the age of ___.
       a. 30   b. 45   c. 60

4. In bad weather, people had to wear shoes made of ___.
       a. leather   b. cloth   c. wood

5. About ___ of all children died before they were five years old.
       a. a third   b. a quarter   c. half

6. Women did many jobs, but they couldn't work as ___.
       a. doctors   b. sailors   c. shoemakers

7. The average family had ___ living children.
       a. five   b. eight   c. ten

8. People used ___ to eat their dinner.
       a. knives   b. forks   c. their fingers

Answers: 1b, 2c, 3a, 4c, 5c, 6b, 7a, 8c

b Emilie is giving the volunteers a talk on the history of the village. Listen and fill in the missing information.

CD T-15

No one knows exactly how old Saint-Marc is. The earliest artifacts we've found are coins and pottery from the Roman times.

By the Middle Ages, it had become quite a large town, with about (1) _____ people. It was very wealthy because it was located in a rich wine-producing area. It had at least eight (2) _____, and many streets of stone or wooden houses. Most of the houses had a shop on the ground floor, and the family lived upstairs. Wine from the region was sold as far away as (3) _____.

In 1458, an earthquake hit Saint-Marc. A number of the old stone buildings were destroyed, and people were afraid to live there. The earthquake also made the (4) _____ dry up, and the town lost all its water. Life here became very difficult, and more and more people left the town. By (5) _____, all the buildings had been abandoned. Farmers let their cows and sheep use the area, and carried away some of the stones to use in new (6) _____. Most people in the area forgot that a large town had been here. In 1993 a (7) _____ at the University of Paris got interested in the site, and his students began excavating it. They were surprised to learn that Saint-Marc had once been the (8) _____ town in the area.

c Heritage Corps started working in the village in 1995. The village was in very bad condition then. Look at the picture and write sentences like the example, using the past perfect tense.

1. *When they started working there, many of the stone buildings had fallen down.*
2. _____
3. _____
4. _____
5. _____

d Fill in the correct form of the verb, simple past or past perfect.

1. I _____ (be, not) hungry for dinner because I _____ (eat) a sandwich after class.
2. Graciela _____ (speak, never) English before she _____ (go) to Canada on vacation last summer.
3. By the time the baseball game _____ (start), the rain _____ (stop), so all the fans _____ (be) happy.
4. When I _____ (apply) to Heritage Corps, the organization _____ (receive, already) hundreds of applications.
5. I _____ (not, see) my cousin in many years when I _____ (meet) him at a holiday party.
6. Estela _____ (feel) very nervous when she _____ (arrive) in Saint-Marc because she _____ (do, never) volunteer work before.

e Emilie's team is planning the Saint-Marc Visitor Center. It will have rooms for five displays. Which displays should the center have? Read the list and add two ideas of your own.

food from the Middle Ages	religion in the Middle Ages	tools from different jobs
history of winemaking	clothes from the Middle Ages	_____
kings and queens of France	furniture from 1250	_____

f Choose five topics for displays and decide which display should be the largest. Use expressions from this box to manage your discussion.

Encouraging people to talk	Bringing people in	Finishing up the discussion
Who has an idea about that? Does anyone else have a suggestion?	Elena, what do you think? Luis, do you want to add anything?	We have only five minutes left. We need to move along.

g Take turns explaining your group's decision and reasons to the class.

Lesson 3

I'd be glad to

a Emilie is talking to volunteers on her team about projects. Read the conversation and write the underlined expressions in the correct column.

Emilie: So, we've decided to start with the display of objects found in the Le Blanc House. First, we need to build the display cases. Margo, <u>would you be willing to</u> take charge of that project? We'll get two or three people to help you.

Margo: <u>I'd be glad to</u>. That sounds like a fun project.

Emilie: The next thing we need is a list of all the displays. Brandon, <u>would you please</u> start working on that this afternoon?

Brandon: <u>Of course</u>. When do you need it?

Emilie: The team leaders are having a meeting at 9:00 tomorrow, so I'll need it before then.

Brandon: <u>Do you want me to</u> show you some ideas we had? Some of us were talking about it last night.

Emilie: <u>Yes, I'd appreciate that</u>. Now, as we discussed, all the displays will have labels in English, French,
and German.

Andreas: <u>Would you like me</u> to translate them into German?

Emilie: <u>That would be great</u>.

Requesting someone to do something	Responding to a request	Offering to do something	Responding to an offer
Please	Sure.	Would you like any help with	Great!
Can you please	Certainly.		
Can I ask you to	I'm afraid I can't (because . . .)		
————————	————————	————————	————————
————————	————————	————————	————————

b What would you say? Practice these conversations with a partner.

1. Your co-worker is carrying a large, heavy box.
2. A foreign tourist in the history museum is standing in front of a display looking up words in a bilingual dictionary.
3. It's very cold in the room. The window is open.
4. Two visitors are taking pictures of each other at a historical park in your country.

c Role-play these situations in groups. Practice the expressions from the chart.

Situation 1

Your group is in charge of planning a class trip to a historical site near your town. One group member is the committee chair.

Situation 2

Your group wants to produce a class magazine with articles and photos by the students. One group member is the editor.

d Emilie's team members have written information panels for the displays in the house. Read the first panel and answer the questions.

Museum

A strong earthquake hit the village of Saint-Marc on April 1, 1458. It happened at about 8:00 in the morning, one of the busiest times of the day. When the earthquake started, craftsmen were working in their shops, housewives were going to the market, and children were studying their lessons or playing in the garden. Suddenly, the ground began to shake. Some people screamed and cried, while others ran to the church and prayed. Many families left their homes and never came back

1. What were people doing when the earthquake started? _____,
   _____, _____, _____

2. What did people do while the ground was shaking? _____,
   _____, _____, _____

3. Which verb tense is used to talk about longer actions? _____

4. Which verb tense is used to talk about shorter, interrupted actions? _____

e Read the next panel and fill in the correct form of each verb.

When the earthquake (1) _____ (start), all of the members of the LeBlanc family (2) _____ (work) in the wine shop downstairs. The father of the family, Roger LeBlanc, (3) _____ (write) in the record book and his three sons (4) _____ (put) wine into bottles. A page from the record book is on the left. The earthquake (5) _____ (destroy) the front wall of the shop, and (6) _____ (start) a fire upstairs in the kitchen. While she (7) _____ (escape) from the shop, Marie LeBlanc, the mother of the family, (8) _____ (drop) a bag of money and keys. You can see it in this display.

 f With your group, choose an important news event in the last ten years that you all remember. Then talk about these questions.

1. What happened?
2. What were you doing when you got the news? How did you find out what happened?
3. What did you do after you heard the news? Why?

■ Lesson 4

At home in 1250 A.D.

a What was life like in your country one hundred years ago? Five hundred years ago? What do you know about people's houses, food, and clothes at those times?

b Emilie and the volunteers have written a brochure for visitors to the Le Blanc House. Read the brochure on page 51 and try to work out the meanings of the words in bold from their context.

c Find words in bold in the reading with these meanings.

1. large pieces of wood from a tree _____
2. large wooden boxes for clothes, dishes, etc. _____
3. not discovered yet _____
4. paper made from animal skin _____
5. a building for horses _____
6. workers who cook and clean a family's house _____
7. the same _____
8. ceramic pieces _____
9. very large wooden containers for water_____
10. a place to get water from the ground _____

d Answer *T* for *True* or *F* for *False*. Correct the *false* statements.

1.	Europeans in the Middle Ages worked more days than we do now.	T	F
2.	Their houses had a lot of furniture.	T	F
3.	Rooms didn't have carpet on the floor.	T	F
4.	Shops and homes were in different buildings.	T	F
5.	People in towns grew food in gardens behind their houses.	T	F
6.	People ate many different kinds of vegetables.	T	F
7.	Most food was very simple.	T	F
8.	People often felt cold inside their houses.	T	F

e From the reading, list these things. Compare your answers with a partner's.

1. Three things about life in Medieval Europe that surprised you
2. Three things about life in Medieval Europe that you would enjoy
3. Three things about life in Medieval Europe that you would hate

f Discuss these questions.

1. How is life today easier than life in the past? How is it harder?
2. If you could live at any time and place in the past, which time and place would you choose? Why?

At home in 1250 A.D.

Life in a French town in 1250 wasn't very comfortable, even for wealthy merchants like the Le Blanc family. The houses of rich and poor people looked almost **identical** from the outside. All were very narrow and four stories tall. Inside, the houses were very different. In a poor neighborhood, one house was shared by many families, each living in only one room. In a rich neighborhood, one family used the whole house.

In a merchant family's house, the first floor was a place of business, while the family lived on the second and third floors. The **servants** lived in small, dark rooms on the top floor, under the roof. Behind the house were a **stable** and storage rooms for the business, and there was a garden that produced vegetables and herbs for the family's kitchen.

Family members spent most of the day working in the shop and the workrooms on the first floor. Upstairs, the largest room was called the solar. In the middle of this large hall was a fireplace where a fire was constantly burning. Even in daytime, most of the light came from the fire, because the windows were very small and covered with **parchment**. There was an oil lamp that was used only at night.

The solar was used as both a living room and a dining room, but it was bare and cold. Its walls were covered with painted cloth, but this didn't keep the room very warm. The floor was made of **tile**. There were only a few simple pieces of furniture, including cupboards and **chests**. At meal times, a long table was made by putting boards across two stands, and the family members sat on benches.

The kitchen was behind the solar. The head cook was always a man, and he had many young boys to help him. The center of the kitchen was a huge fireplace that burned **logs** up to a meter long. This fireplace was used for cooking, and to heat water for washing. Pots, pans, and cooking utensils hung on the walls and ceiling, and there was a special cabinet for spices. It was always kept locked, because they were so expensive.

All food was cooked over the fire, so preparing a meal took a long time. Towns had outdoor markets that sold many kinds of meat, fish, cheese, vegetables, and cakes. Cooks used very complicated recipes, but many common foods today were **unknown** then. Europeans in the Middles Ages didn't have chocolate, tomatoes, rice, potatoes, corn, or pasta — and there was no tea or coffee, either!

On the third floor were the bedrooms. Because of the cold, people slept in beds filled with straw, with thick curtains hanging on the sides. To keep insects out of the beds, the family sprinkled flowers and herbs in them. The only other furniture was a chest for clothes.

It wasn't easy keeping clean in these conditions. Water came from a **well** in the garden, and the servants carried it into the house. The toilet was an outhouse in the garden. When people wanted a bath, they had to boil the water in the kitchen. Servants washed clothes by hand in big wooden **tubs** with home-made soap.

Though life was hard, people actually had more days off from work than we do. On "holy days," people went to church, and work was not allowed. There were other holidays such as Mid-Summer Day, and Saint-Marc had trade fairs with merchants from many countries and entertainment by actors and musicians.

Lesson 5

It must have been uncomfortable

 a Look at the picture and write these sentences in the correct column. Then write two more sentences of your own.

They <u>might have</u> had other clothes for hot weather.
They <u>could have</u> put on their best clothes just for this picture.
Those clothes <u>must have</u> been really uncomfortable.
They <u>couldn't have</u> worn those shoes to walk in!

Things you feel sure about:

_____

_____

_____

Things you are guessing about:

_____

_____

_____

Things that are possible:

_____

_____

_____

Things that are not possible:

_____

_____

_____

 b With a partner, talk about this picture using _might have / must have / could have / couldn't have._

c Emilie is giving an oral report at the Team Leaders' meeting. Fill in the correct form of each verb *(simple past, past continuous, past perfect, present perfect, or modal perfect)*. There may be more than one correct answer.

I'm going to tell you about our work this month, which (1) _____ (be) very exciting. Last month, I (2) _____ (talk) about our plan for the displays in the visitor center, but we (3) _____ (finish, not) working on them yet.

On July 12, we (4) _____ (install) the display cases when I (5) _____ (hear) Andreas shouting. He (6) _____ (move) some stones when he (7) _____ (notice) a hollow space under the floor! We (8) _____ (stop) working immediately, and (9) _____ (call) the archaeology team. They (10) _____ (discover) a small hidden storage room under the house. While they (11) _____ (dig), they (12) _____ (uncover) a lot of coins and two beautiful gold bracelets. The family (13) _____ (use) the place to hide money and jewelry before the earthquake (14) _____ (bury) it. They also (15) _____ (find) children's toys down there. They think that small children in the Le Blanc family (16) _____ (play) down in the storage room sometimes.

Later, after the excavation, we (17) _____ (have) a meeting to discuss our plans. We (18) _____ (decide) to put a glass window in the floor to let visitors see the hidden room. Now we (19) _____ (almost finish) cleaning the objects we found down there. Next week, we plan to finish installing the display cases. In conclusion, despite the delays we are very pleased with our work this month.

d Compare your answers with a partner's and explain why you used each tense.

e Emilie's oral report is an example of narration — talking about a series of events in the past. Look back at the report and fill in the expressions she used for these things. Which expressions are more formal? Which are informal?

Introducing the narration	Telling when something happened	Showing the sequence of events	Concluding the narration
I'm going to discuss Have I ever told you about _____	In 1952 When I was fifteen Last summer _____	First To start with Next Then After that _____	So, in the end To summarize Finally _____

f Choose one of these topics and narrate the story to your partner. While you listen to your partner, use some of the expressions for reacting to a story.

1. An event that changed the world
2. Your most important decision
3. An interesting story from your country's history
4. Your most frightening experience

Reacting to a story
Wow!
Really?
What happened then?
What did you do next?

Lesson 6

Messages from the past

 a Read these quotations about history and work out their meanings, using a dictionary as necessary. Write what they mean in your notebook.

> *There is history in all men's lives.*
> -- William Shakespeare, English playwright
>
> *The past is not dead. In fact, it's not even past.*
> --William Faulkner, American novelist
>
> *We learn from history that we do not learn from history.*
> -- Georg Friedrich Hegel, German philosopher
>
> *History never looks like history when you are living through it.*
> --John Gardner, American novelist
>
> *Those who cannot remember the past are condemned to repeat it.*
> --George Santayana, Spanish-American philosopher
>
> *You can never plan the future by the past.*
> --Edmund Burke, English philosopher
>
> *Things that are done, it is needless to speak about.*
> --Confucius, Chinese philosopher
>
> *History is bunk!*
> -- Henry Ford, American industrialist

b Which of the quotations do you agree with? Which do you disagree with?

c Write a paragraph about one of the quotations in Exercise **a**. Explain its meaning and tell why you agree or disagree with it. Give examples.

_____

_____

_____

_____

_____

_____

d Discuss these questions with a partner.

1. What is the oldest thing in your house right now? What is its story? Do you still use it?
2. Do you like to keep a lot of old things, or do you usually throw them away? Why?

e Imagine that archaeologists 500 years from now are excavating your city and they find these objects. Role-play what they would say.

a skateboard: People must have used it for transportation. They must have sat on it.

f Read this article and answer the questions.

Time Capsules: Messages from the Past

A time capsule is a container filled with things that show what life was like at a particular time. It is stored for a fixed period — for example, 100 years — and then opened again. Time capsules are often put into the walls of new buildings, or they may be buried in the ground. They usually contain photos, letters, newspapers, and objects from everyday life. A carefully made time capsule preserves a living record of history and gives people a voice into the future.

According to the International Time Capsule Society, there are about 10,000 time capsules in the world. However, many of them have been lost or forgotten. For example, in Blackpool, Lancashire, England, a time capsule was included in the Blackpool Tower when it was built in the late 1800s. Unfortunately, no one recorded the exact location. When people searched for it 100 years later, they were unable to find it. The International Time Capsule Society now keeps an official record of time capsules around the world to avoid problems like this in the future.

1. Why do people make time capsules? _____

_____

2. What is inside a time capsule? _____

_____

g The government is planning a new park in your city, and they have asked your committee to design a monument with a time capsule inside it. The monument will be a symbol of life in your country now, and it will be five meters tall. Work together to design the monument.

1. Choose a shape for your monument. What does it mean?
2. Choose three symbols to describe life today that will be put on the outside.
3. Choose ten things to put inside the time capsule which will be opened 100 years from now. These things should describe what life is like today.
4. With the group, draw a picture of your monument on a large piece of paper.

h Take turns telling the class about your monument and the items you chose for the time capsule. Explain your decisions.

Team Project 4

Task:
Write a historical guide to your city

The Local History Society has asked your team to write a historical guide to your city (or your region) for foreign visitors. The brochure will be distributed at hotels and tourist offices.

With your team, produce a brochure that contains the following information:

1. A page introducing the history of your city or region. Foreign visitors may not be familiar with your country's history, so be sure to include explanations that they will understand.

2. Pages on interesting places to visit. Each group member should write one page. For each place, tell visitors about the history of the place, what they will see there, and why it's important.

3. A map that shows the location of each place.

   Illustrate your brochure with drawings or photographs, and make an attractive cover that will be interesting for foreign tourists.

56 Team Project 4

Unit 5

Social Science

a Think about positive and negative things about your education up to now. Then discuss these questions.

1. Where did you go to secondary school? What was your school like?
2. What did you like most about your school? What did you dislike most?
3. If you could change one thing about the educational system in your country, what would you change?
4. What ideas have you heard for improving education in your country? Do you think they would work?

b Listen to the radio program and complete the profile.

CD
T-16

> **Name:** Naomi Yoshida
> **Works for:** Institute for (1) _____,
> part of Osaka _____
> **Profession:** (2) _____
> **Special field:** comparative (3) _____
> **Current project:** compare people's ideas about
> (4)_____ in different countries
> **Research question:** (5) _____
> _____?
> **Number of countries in the study:** (6) _____
> **Countries she will visit:** (7) _____, _____
> **Amount of time in each country:** (8) _____

c Naomi is planning her trip. Match the expressions for things she needs to do. Then discuss what she should do first, and what she should do last.

1. renew ___   a. her suitcases
2. make ___   b. her flights
3. exchange ___   c. some money
4. buy ___   d. a plane ticket
5. pack ___   e. all the lights
6. confirm ___   f. her passport
7. change ___   g. hotel reservations
8. turn off ___   h. her voice mail message

d Talk about these questions.

1. Do you know anyone who travels for their work? What do they do? Where do they travel?
2. What careers can you think of that require travel?
3. Would you like to have a job that requires you to travel? Why or why not?

e Naomi is in a café talking about her trip with a friend from work. Read their conversation, paying attention to the use of *will* and *going to*.

Susan: What are you **going to** do in your free time on your trip? (1) ___

Naomi: Well, in Seoul I'm **going to** visit some of the palaces, and go shopping in the outdoor market. (2) ___ In Taipei, I'm **going to** eat dinner in a different restaurant every night. (3) ___

Susan: Do you think you could bring back some postcards for my son's collection? That always makes him so happy.

Naomi: I **will**. (4) ___ I **won't** forget! (5) ___

Susan: You're going to have such an interesting trip! (6) ___

Naomi: I hope so! I'm looking forward to talking with people there. I think Korea and Taiwan **will** be very important countries in education in the future. (7) ___

Susan: Wow, look at the sky! It's **going to** rain any minute. (8) ___ Maybe we should pay and start walking to the subway.

Naomi: You're right. **I'll** ask for the bill. (9) ___

f Write the future form that is used for each purpose. Then write the letter after each sentence in Exercise **e**.

a. to make a serious promise _____

b. to talk about something you've already decided to do _____

c. to make a prediction _____

d. to make a serious prediction _____

e. to predict something that will happen very soon or immediately _____

f. to make a quick decision _____

g Write notes about your predictions, plans, and promises below.

1. predictions about changes in your school ten years from now:
   a. _____ b. _____ c. _____
2. your plans for next weekend:
   a. _____ b. _____ c. _____
3. predictions about life in your country ten years from now:
   a. _____ b. _____ c. _____
4. promises you make to your English teacher:
   a. _____ b. _____ c. _____

h Take turns asking and telling about the things you listed in Exercise **g**. Use *will* or *going to* as appropriate.

Lesson 2

I'm very happy to be here

a Naomi has just arrived at the airport in Seoul. Write numbers to put the conversation in order. Then practice with a partner.

___ **Prof. Park:** Well, tomorrow we'll take you on a city tour, and then the next day we'll visit some schools.

_1_ **Prof. Park:** Are you Dr. Yoshida?

___ **Prof. Park:** I'm glad to hear that. Have you been to Seoul before?

___ **Prof. Park:** We all hope you'll enjoy your stay here.

___ **Prof. Park:** I'm Professor Park Young-jun, from Shilla University. Welcome!

___ **Prof. Park:** Did you have a good flight?

___ **Naomi:** That sounds interesting.

___ **Naomi:** Yes, I am.

___ **Naomi:** Yes, but that was ten years ago. I've heard that the city has changed a lot.

___ **Naomi:** Thank you! I'm very happy to be here.

___ **Naomi:** Yes, I did. Everything went very well.

___ **Naomi:** I'm sure I will!

b Role-play these situations.

Situation 1
Student A: You are an American teacher. You have come to work at an international school in this city.
Student B: You are the director of the school. Meet the visitor at the airport and welcome him/her to your city.

Situation 2
Student A: You are a famous professor of sociology. You have come to this city to give a lecture at an important conference.
Student B: You are the assistant to the conference chairman. Meet the teacher at the airport and introduce him/her to your city.

c Read the report about education in South Korea on page 61.

d Read the statements about the report and answer *T* for *True*, *F* for *False*, or *NI* for *No Information*.

1.	Korean students attend school for 12 years before university.	T	F	NI
2.	Only girls have to wear school uniforms.	T	F	NI
3.	The most important universities are in the capital.	T	F	NI
4.	It's difficult to get good grades in a Korean university.	T	F	NI
5.	Korean children have classes six days a week.	T	F	NI
6.	The high school entrance exam is extremely difficult.	T	F	NI
7.	The school day is seven or eight hours long.	T	F	NI
8.	University students graduate after four years.	T	F	NI

The Korean Educational System

South Korean children spend six years in elementary school, three years in middle school, and three years in high school. Students don't change classrooms between periods — instead, the teachers move to different rooms. And every day at school, the students are required to clean their own classrooms.

For most Korean children, the school day from Monday to Friday includes six to seven 50-minute classes a day. There is a 10-minute break in between, when teachers change classes, with an hour for lunch. On Saturday, students have classes in the morning. Each class has about 40-50 students, and each student has an identification number.

Students at most public schools must wear uniforms and a tag with their name, grade, and class number. The girls' skirts must be long, and there are very strict rules about hair styles and even hair color for both boys and girls.

Korean students compete against each other for the best grades, and high school is especially difficult. To enter a top-level university, students must get a high score on the university entrance exam. One proverb says: "Sleep four hours a night and you'll pass the exam; sleep five hours a night and you'll fail." Once students are in the university, their classes are easy and nearly all students pass.

 e Discuss the questions with a partner.

1. How is the system in Korea similar to the system in your country? How is it different?
2. Would any aspects of the Korean system work well in your country? Why or why not?

f Look at these sentences and answer the questions.

1. Which future form is used to talk about plans we've made? _____
2. Which future form is used to talk about fixed schedules? _____

> *Tomorrow night, I'm seeing a movie with my friends. It starts at 8:00. I'm meeting my friends outside the theater.*

 g Read Naomi's schedule and tell a partner about her activities next week.

Monday	Tuesday	Wednesday	Thursday	Friday	Saturday	Sunday
visit middle school		morning: interview students	talk to Parents' Association	write report		Train to Pusan — 2 p.m.
	concert at National Theater — 7:30 p.m.	afternoon: visit high school			shopping at dept. stores	

Lesson 3
Gathering information

a Naomi is visiting King Sejong High School in Korea and talking to the principal, Dr. Kim. Read their conversation and underline the phrases that make Naomi's questions more polite.

Naomi: I'd like to know who King Sejong was. He must have been important in Korean history if your school is named after him.

Dr. Kim: He certainly was! He invented our Korean alphabet.

Naomi: That's interesting. Do you know when he did that?

Dr. Kim: It was in the fifteenth century. So, what else can I tell you about our school?

Naomi: Well, I was wondering how many students are in each class.

Dr. Kim: There are about forty students, but we are hiring more teachers so the classes will be smaller.

Naomi: Can you tell me whether the students like smaller classes?

Dr. Kim: I'm not sure, but you can ask them when you interview them.

b Complete the chart. Circle the correct answer to each question in Exercise **a**. Then circle the correct answer in the definitions below.

Indirect question	Direct question
1. I'd like to know who King Sejong was.	*Who was King Sejong?*
2. Do you know when he did that?	
3. I was wondering how many students are in each class.	
4. Can you tell me whether the students like smaller classes?	

1. For indirect questions, use (question / statement) word order.
2. Indirect questions are more (formal / informal) than direct questions.
3. For indirect yes/no questions, we use (whether / if / that).

c Rewrite Naomi's questions to make them more polite. Use the cues in parentheses.

1. Where's Ms. Chun's office? (can you tell me)

   _____

2. How many students attend this school? (do you know)

   _____

3. Where do the students eat their lunch? (I'd like to know)

   _____

4. Can I take a picture of this classroom? (I was wondering)

   _____

5. How much homework do the students have every night? (I'd like to know)

   _____

6. Do the students like their uniforms? (do you know)

   _____

d Imagine that you are a foreign researcher gathering information about schools in this country. Think of information you would like to get about the topics below. Plan your questions. Don't write them down.

the building	the classes
the teachers	the students

e Role-play an interview using the questions from Exercise **d**. Then change roles and practice again.

Student A: You are the researcher. Ask your questions politely.
Student B: You are the principal / director of the school. (Talk about a school that you attended in the past.)

CD
T-17

f Naomi is interviewing students and parents in another Korean city about their opinions on schools. Listen and complete her notes. Then tell a partner what you think about each idea.

Jae-Hak
student at (1) _____
most important thing is (2) _____
you learn to get along with (3) _____

Myoung-Hee
student at (1) _____
most important thing is (2) _____
they should reward (3) _____ for (4) _____
and encourage them to (5) _____

Mrs. Shin
most important thing is (1) _____
son is a (2) _____ student at a school with
(3) _____
It's much more (4) _____

g With your group, write a list of ten things that are important for a good school.

h Work individually to rank them here in order from most to least important.

1. _____
2. _____
3. _____
4. _____
5. _____

6. _____
7. _____
8. _____
9. _____
10. _____

Lesson 4

How good are our schools

a Read this information and answer the questions.

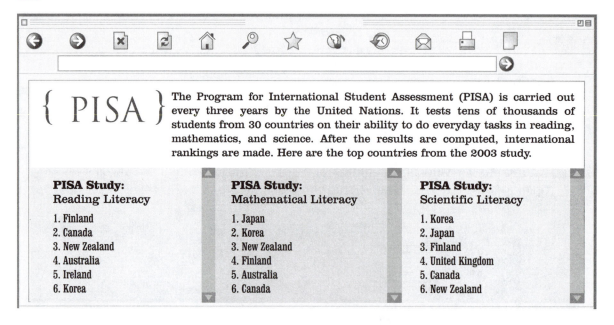

{ PISA } The Program for International Student Assessment (PISA) is carried out every three years by the United Nations. It tests tens of thousands of students from 30 countries on their ability to do everyday tasks in reading, mathematics, and science. After the results are computed, international rankings are made. Here are the top countries from the 2003 study.

PISA Study:
Reading Literacy

1. Finland
2. Canada
3. New Zealand
4. Australia
5. Ireland
6. Korea

PISA Study:
Mathematical Literacy

1. Japan
2. Korea
3. New Zealand
4. Finland
5. Australia
6. Canada

PISA Study:
Scientific Literacy

1. Korea
2. Japan
3. Finland
4. United Kingdom
5. Canada
6. New Zealand

1. Does your country appear on the list? If not, where do you think it would be in the list of all 30 countries?
2. Do you think this is a good way to compare schools in different countries? Why or why not?

b Read the two responses on page 65 to the information above.

c Read the statements about the responses and mark who would agree with them.

	Mr. Curtis	Dr. Abbas	Both	Neither
1. International tests are a good way to measure the quality of schools.				
2. Our country needs to spend more money for schools.				
3. The quality of teachers in our country is not high enough.				
4. A good school is the same in every country.				
5. Children learn best in a strict environment.				
6. Schools should be different in different cultures.				
7. Children have too many tests in school.				
8. Our schools are actually some of the best in the world.				

d Which of these statements do you agree with? Which do you disagree with? Why? Compare your opinions with a partner's.

Learn from the Best

by John H. Curtis, President,
Parents for Better Schools

Our schools have just received their report card — and the grades are not good. When results of an international test called the Program for International Student Assessment (PISA) were released, our country wasn't in the top ten. Or even the top twenty.

It's not surprising to see which nations are on the top of the list: Asian countries such as Singapore, South Korea, Taiwan, and Japan, where schools are strict and all children are expected to learn. School days are long, there are frequent exams, and there are no after-school clubs or sports.

Some people don't understand why our schools got such poor results. We spend a higher percentage of the national budget on education than most of the top countries. Our students also spend longer in class. The average of the 30 wealthiest countries is 929 hours per year, while our students spend over 1000 hours in class. But what are they learning?

There are several reasons for the problem. One is the poor quality of our teachers, who are badly trained. But the most important is the lack of family pressure on children to study. If students in South Korea, Japan, or Singapore come home with a failing grade, they will be punished. In our country, parents don't care.

We need to change this attitude and make study the number one priority for every child. And we also need to analyze what has been so successful in the top-ranked countries and use this information to reform our schools.

Schools that Are Right for Us

by Dr. Maryam Abbas, Professor of Education, Pacific University

It's true that our country was not on the top of the list in the PISA study — but we shouldn't be too worried about that.

You can't measure the quality of schools by giving a test with paper and pencil. You can test children's ability to solve math problems, or to understand what they read. But do these children know how to work together with other people? Can they use their creativity and imagination? Do they know and love the traditions of their country? Schools teach a lot of important things that can't be tested.

It's true that our schools have some serious problems. Many of our classrooms have far too many students, and the differences in facilities between city and rural schools are too great. We need to build more schools as soon as possible to improve this situation. We also need to increase salaries in our school system and encourage our most talented university graduates to become teachers.

But we can't just use the Japanese, Canadian, or Finnish systems as a model for our country's schools. We have our own traditions and ways of thinking, which are very different from the ones in these "top ranked" countries. You can't just import an educational system, the way you can import cars or soft drinks.

We need to develop our own system that fits our culture and our children. Every country is different. They all want the best for their children, and they all need to find their own solutions to the problems they face in education.

Lesson 5

How is your research going

a Match the name of the expert with the field of study.

1. sociologist ___
2. psychologist ___
3. anthropologist ___
4. economist ___
5. political scientist ___

a. different cultures and their customs
b. the human mind and emotions
c. how different kinds of government work
d. how people live together in society
e. the system of money and business

b Look at the questions below. Decide which type of social scientist would study them. Write each question in the correct box.

1. How can parents have a better relationship with their children?
2. Will people buy more cars if the price is lower?
3. Who was our country's most popular president?
4. What can our country do to reduce unemployment?
5. Do teenagers think the future will be better or worse than now?
6. Who did elderly people vote for in the last election?
7. How do people in Nigeria find a husband or a wife?
8. Why are some people happier than others?
9. Why do more married women have jobs today?
10. How do native people live in the desert in Australia?

sociologist
psychologist
anthropologist
economist
political scientist

c Naomi is attending a reception for visiting researchers in Seoul. She is talking to three other social scientists. Listen to what they say, and identify each person's field.

CD
T-18

1. anthropologist ____   psychologist ____   economist ____
2. sociologist ____   political scientist ____   psychologist ____
3. political scientist ____   economist ____   sociologist ____

d Read the article.

Making Small Talk

Small talk means pleasant conversation about things that aren't very important. North Americans often make small talk with people such as business acquaintances, neighbors, or others that they don't know very well. They even make small talk while waiting for a bus or standing in line, just to pass the time or be friendly. In North America, one very common topic for small talk with strangers is the weather. You can start a conversation just by saying, "It's really hot today, isn't it?"

e Which of these are good topics for small talk in your country? Which are not suitable? Do you think this is similar or different in other countries?

___ the weather	___ sports	___ news events	___ your work
___ TV programs	___ your age	___ your school	___ your clothes
___ your family	___ politics	___ your salary	___ your health

f On the plane to Taipei, Naomi is talking to the woman seated next to her. Read their conversation and fill in the correct future forms: *simple present, present continuous, will,* or *going to*.

In-sook: This rain is terrible, isn't it?

Naomi: Yes, I was afraid the plane would be delayed for a long time . . . I'm a little worried because a colleague (1) _____ (meet) me in Taipei.

In-sook: Are you going there for your work?

Naomi: Yes, I am. I (2) _____ (spend) a month in Taiwan doing research.

In-sook: Really? What's your research about?

Naomi: I'm a sociologist. I'm studying people's opinions in different countries about what makes a good school.

In-sook: That sounds interesting! How (3) _____ (study) that?

Naomi: I (4) _____ (talk) to parents and students at different schools, and write a report about their ideas.

In-sook: (5) _____ (stay) in Taipei for a whole month?

Naomi: No, just for a week. Next Friday I (6) _____ (go) to Taichung for a week, and then I (7) _____ (take) the train to Kaohsiung. After that, I (8) _____ (interview) people in several small towns, but I don't know where yet.

In-sook: (9) _____ (have) any time to do some sightseeing?

Naomi: At the end of the trip I (10) _____ (have) three free days. I (11) _____ (visit) the famous temples in Tainan, and go to the beach in Kenting.

g  Role-play these conversations with a partner.

Situation 1
You are a teacher at your school. At a reception, you meet a foreign scientist who is doing research in your country.

Situation 2
You are sitting on a plane next to a foreign tourist who is very interested in your country.

Lesson 6

The results of our survey show . . .

a Review the future verb forms and their meanings. Then read the sentences and cross out the future verb forms that *don't* make a correct sentence (there might be 1, 2, 3, or 4 correct answers). Talk about the differences in meaning in the correct sentences.

1. It _____ tomorrow.
   a. rains   b. is raining   c. will rain   d. is going to rain

2. We don't have any more corn flakes. I _____ some when I go to the store.
   a. buy   b. am buying   c. will buy   d. am going to buy

3. "I promise I _____ my report tomorrow," Naomi said to her boss.
   a. send   b. am sending   c. will send   d. am going to send

4. I need to leave my hotel at 7:00 because the concert _____ at 8:00 and I don't want to be late.
   a. starts   b. is starting   c. will start   d. is going to start

5. On Saturday, I _____ to Taipei to meet with people in the Ministry of Education.
   a. go   b. am going   c. will go   d. am going to go

b Work in groups of four members to choose a social science topic, such as elderly people or the economy. With your group, plan two survey questions.

> *Where is the best place for elderly people to live—with their children, in their own home, or in a senior citizens' home?*

> *In your opinion, what is the biggest economic problem in our country today?*

c Give your survey to five other people (classmates, other students in your school, or friends). Write down all the answers you receive.

d With your group, combine all the information and discuss what it means. Then plan a presentation for the class. Each group member should give one part of the presentation.

Student 1: Introduction: your questions and why you chose them
Student 2: The answers to the first question
Student 3: The answers to the second question
Student 4: Conclusion: what these answers mean

Tips for giving a presentation

- Speak in a voice that's slightly louder than normal so that everyone in your audience can hear you.
- Use notes to help you remember the important points, but don't just read your presentation from the paper.
- Look at different members of the audience as you speak. This eye contact will make your listeners more interested in your presentation.

e Give your presentation to the class. Answer any questions from the audience.

f Read the notes from Naomi's research in Korea.

Cities visited: *Seoul, Pusan, Kwangju*
People interviewed: *57 (27 parents, 30 students)*
Number of students: *middle school: 8, high school: 20, university: 2*
Some results:

Parents' responses	Students' responses
Most important factors for a good school: 1. good teachers 2. individual help for students 3. pleasant atmosphere 4. good preparation for exams 5. comfortable building	**Most important factors for a good school:** 1. good teachers 2. comfortable building 3. interesting classes 4. good lunches 5. nice uniforms
Biggest problems in present schools: 1. class size too large 2. too much pressure from exams 3. old school buildings 4. not enough contact between parents and teachers 5. low-quality textbooks	**Biggest problems in present schools:** 1. boring teachers 2. too much homework 3. too much pressure from exams 4. bad lunches 5. not enough free time

g Naomi is writing a summary of her research in Korea to send to the director of the Institute for Global Education. Use the information from the chart to complete her summary.

For our survey, we interviewed (1) _____ people in three different (2) _____ in Korea. Of the people we talked to, 27 were (3) _____ and (4) _____ were students. We talked with students from three educational levels: (5) _____, _____, and _____.
One question that we asked was, "What (6) _____ _____?" For both (7) _____ and (8) _____, the most common answer was (9) "_____." Parents said the second most important thing was (10) _____, while students said that it was (11) _____.
Another question was, "What are the biggest problems in present schools?" Parents **think that** (12)_____ are the biggest problem, while students **feel that** (13) _____ are the worst.
From this we can see that there are interesting similarities in the answers of parents and students. Both **believe that** (14) _____ and (15) _____ are important for a good school. But there are also many differences. For example, students think that (16) _____ and (17) _____ are very important, but parents don't care much about them. The results of our survey show that both parents and students have strong ideas about what makes a good school.

Task:

Design the ideal school

Your team has decided to enter an international competition to design the ideal school building. This project can be for any level: kindergarten, elementary, middle, or high school, university, or a specialized school like a language institute.

With your team:

1. Choose the type of school that you want to design.

2. Consider the ideas in this unit, and your own ideas about the ideal school. Think about features of the whole building and the features of each classroom.

3. Do additional research on the Internet. Take notes.

4. Compare notes and consolidate the information you have gathered. Come to a consensus.

5. On a large sheet of paper, make a poster explaining the features of your ideal school in words and pictures.

6. Present your school and its features to the class.

Review 1

A Rewrite this conversation to make it more polite.

Student: Hi, Professor Blake. Are you doing anything now?

_____

Professor: No. What's up?

_____

Student: Your class today was really confusing. I couldn't understand anything.

_____

Professor: Did you read the assignment before class?

_____

Student: I tried to, but it was too hard.

_____

Professor: It's important. Read it again. Then come back and ask me questions.

_____

Student: OK. Bye.

_____

Professor: Bye.

_____

B Complete these _conditional_ sentences with your own ideas.

1. If I get a good grade for this course, _____.
2. _____, people in my country will be really happy.
3. _____ if our teacher gives us a difficult test.
4. My family will be very upset _____.
5. If I have time tonight, _____.
6. _____ life in this city will be better.

C Complete the sentence with the correct form of the verb in the _simple past_ or _present perfect_.

1. I _____ (read, not) any good books in a long time.
2. Really? I _____ (read) a great book last week—_The Story of Philosophy_.
3. Loren _____ (miss) class several times so far this semester.
   She _____ (be) absent yesterday because she has a cold.
4. I _____ (learn) to play chess when I was a child,
   but now I _____ (forget) how to play.
5. We _____ (have, not) any debates in this class until now.
6. Technology _____ (develop) very rapidly in the last twenty years.
7. They _____ (start) learning English more than ten years ago.
8. I _____ (meet) my best friend in elementary school.
   I _____ (know) her for twelve years.

Review 2

A Circle the correct verb form (*gerund* or *infinitive*) in these sentences. Some sentences have two correct answers.

1. I really enjoy (watching / to watch) old movies on TV late at night.
2. After graduation, I plan (taking / to take) a vacation before I start my job.
3. A lot of people dislike (eating / to eat) food that is good for them.
4. I am pretty good at (remembering / to remember) new vocabulary words.
5. Jessica hates (doing / to do) the same thing every day at work.
6. Do you like (getting up / to get up) early in the morning?
7. Kevin hopes (finding / to find) a job in an international company.
8. I want (asking / to ask) you about what happened in class yesterday.
9. We decided (having / to have) our meeting on Friday afternoon.

B Find and correct one mistake in each of these sentences.

1. If I win the lottery, I would give a lot of the money to charity.
2. Where would you went if you could travel anywhere in the world?
3. Dave would enjoy his job more if he didn't had such a noisy office.
4. If I was you, I wouldn't wear jeans to that job interview.
5. Would Erika takes a vacation if she had more money?
6. You would have more energy if you wouldn't eat so much junk food!

C Write advice for a classmate about how to become more proficient in a foreign language.

1. I think it's a good idea _____.
2. I don't think _____.
3. If I were you, _____.
4. Maybe you should _____.
5. If I were you, I wouldn't _____.

D Match the columns to make polite expressions for telephone conversations.

1. Could you please ___   a. that.
2. Sorry, I didn't hear ___   b. to Mr. Simons, please.
3. Could I have ___   c. the Shipping Department, please?
4. I'd like to speak ___   d. a message?
5. Could I leave ___   e. catch your name.
6. Excuse me, I didn't ___   f. spell that?

Review 3

A Complete the chart with the *comparative* and *superlative* forms of each adjective.

	Comparative	Superlative
1. important	_____	_____
2. large	_____	_____
3. easy	_____	_____
4. careful	_____	_____
5. far	_____	_____
6. good	_____	_____
7. relaxing	_____	_____
8. soft	_____	_____
9. fat	_____	_____
10. bad	_____	_____

B Mark each sentence *Active* or *Passive*. Then rewrite it in the other form.

1. A teenaged girl wrote that romance novel.   Active / Passive

   _____

2. The concert was attended by over two thousand people.   Active / Passive

   _____

3. Several companies in Japan produce electric cars.   Active / Passive

   _____

4. The celebrity didn't answer the reporters' questions.   Active / Passive

   _____

5. Several famous paintings were exhibited by the city museum. Active / Passive

   _____

6. Zimbaco's artists are developing new products.   Active / Passive

   _____

7. The announcement by the president didn't surprise me.   Active / Passive

   _____

8. Christmas is celebrated in summer by people in Australia.   Active/ Passive

   _____

C Match the columns to make correct *conditional* sentences.

1. If the weather is good, __   a. I would need to take the bus.
2. If my coworkers were friendlier, __ b. I'll go to the beach this weekend.
3. If I had known you would be there, __ c. I would enjoy my work more.
4. If I'm late for work, __   d. I have to stay at the office until I finish.
5. If I didn't have a car, __   e. I would have gotten a job by now.
6. If I had graduated last year, __   f. I would have gone to the party.

Review 4

A Complete the sentences with the correct form of the verb in the *simple past* or *past perfect*.

1. When I _____ (see) my friend, he _____ (just, get) home from vacation.
   He _____ (be) in London.

2. My apartment _____ (look) terrible because I _____ (clean, not) it
   in a month.

3. I _____ (come) to class late yesterday. When I _____ (open) the door,
   the teacher _____ (already, start) the lesson. I _____ (walk) in
   very quietly!

4. Last night, James _____ (get) home at 1 a.m. His parents
   _____ (go) to bed, so he _____ (turn on, not) the TV.

5. Sandy _____ (invite) me to her party last week, but I _____
   (go, not) because I _____ (already, make) other plans.

B Give two possible reasons for each situation, using *might have / must have / could have / couldn't have*.

1. Luis left work early. He ran to his car and drove away very fast.
   a. _____
   b. _____

2. The woman walked out of the doctor's office with a big smile on her face.
   a. _____
   b. _____

3. When I came home, the living room window was broken.
   a. _____
   b. _____

4. The police officers walked up to the house and knocked on the door.
   a. _____
   b. _____

C Circle the correct form of each verb—*simple past* or *past continuous*.

1. The baby (slept / was sleeping) when his mother (walked / was walking) in.

2. What (did you do / were you doing) yesterday at 8:00? I (called / was calling) you, but you (didn't answer / weren't answering) the phone.

3. Oh, sorry! I (took / was taking) a nap when you (called / were calling), so I (didn't hear / wasn't hearing) my phone.

4. While I (studied / was studying), my brother (turned on / was turning on) his stereo.

5. Klara (drove / was driving) home from work when she (saw / was seeing) an accident.

Review 5

A Match these sentences about future time with their purpose.

1. I'll never forget you. ___
2. I'm going to see a movie tonight. ___
3. You're going to have a great time in Paris. ___
4. In the future, people will take their vacations on the moon. ___
5. The train to Tokyo leaves at 9:15. ___
6. Look at that car—it's going to crash! ___
7. I'll have a chicken sandwich. ___
8. I'm having dinner with my grandparents on Sunday. ___

a. talk about a fixed schedule
b. make a prediction
c. make a serious promise
d. talk about an intention
e. make a quick decision
f. make an important prediction
g. talk about something that will happen very soon or immediately
h. talk about a plan already made

B Complete each sentence with a future verb form.

1. The sky is really dark. It _____ (rain).
2. I'm tired of waiting for the bus. I think I _____ (walk) home.
3. Naomi _____ (leave) for Osaka next Saturday.
4. A hundred years from now, no one _____ (remember) what trees looked like.
5. The art show _____ (open) on September 12.
6. What _____ (you, do) tomorrow after class?
7. I'm tired. I _____ (go) go to bed early tonight.
8. I _____ (always, remember) how much you helped me.

Unit 1

Present perfect vs. simple past

Present perfect	subject + has/ have/ past participle
Affirmative statement	**He has studied** philosophy in his home country. subject + has/have + past participle
Negative statement	**He has not studied** in a foreign country before. subject + has/have + not + past participle
Yes/no questions	**Have you taken** any philosophy courses? has/have + subject + past participle
Wh- questions	**How long has he been** a student here? Wh- word + has/have + subject + past participle

Use the present perfect tense:
- to show that something happened at an unspecified time in the past
- to show that something happened several times in the past
- to show that something started at a specific time in the past and continues now

PRACTICE 1

Mr. and Mrs. Lee are leaving on vacation tonight. Complete their conversation with the correct *present perfect* form of each verb.

Mr. Lee: ___*Have you done*___ all the errands?

Mrs. Lee: No, (1) _____ (finish, not) them yet.

Mr. Lee: You don't have to go to the bank. (2) _____ (already get) some foreign money.

Mrs. Lee: Great! And (3) _____ (pick up) the plane tickets. And (4) _____ (pack) carry-on bags. What about you? (5) _____ (wash) the dishes?

Mr. Lee: No, and (6) _____ (clean, not) the kitchen. But (7) _____ (water) the plants. And (8) _____ (give) our keys to the neighbors.

Mrs. Lee: What about your suitcase? (9) _____ (pack) it?

Mr. Lee: Not yet... but don't worry. There's still lots of time!

PRACTICE 2

Complete the sentence with the correct form of the verb in the *simple past* or *present perfect*.

1. Since we _____ (start) this course, we _____ (finish) one unit.
2. I (eat) _____ at the Italian restaurant many times. I _____ (go) there last week with my family.
3. The weather _____ (be) rainy again yesterday. It _____ (be) rainy every day for a long time!
4. Javier _____ (be, not) to the United States, but he _____ (go) to Canada in 2003.

Real conditionals in the present or future

Condition   **Result**

If + subject + present tense verb	subject + will + verb
If I have time today, If I don't see you tomorrow, If it rains on Saturday,	I'll call my mother I'll send you an e-mail. they won't go to the beach.

Yes/no questions

If + subject + present tense verb, will + subject + verb	Short answer
If you don't have to study, will you go to the movie with me? If you ask your father, will he give you more money? If I invite your brother, will he come to my party?	Yes, I will. No, he won't. Yes, he will.

Wh- questions

If + subject + past tense verb, *wh*- word + will + subject + verb	Answer
If the company offers you a job, what will you do? If our teacher asks why you were absent, what will you say? If the weather is bad this weekend, where will you go?	I'll accept it. I'll say I was sick. I'll stay home.

> **Real conditionals** talk about situations that are real or possible in the present or future.
> The *if* clause can come first or second in the sentence:
>> I'll call my counselor *if I have time today.*
>> Will you go to the movie with me *if you don't have to study?*
>> What will you do *if you hand in the report late?*
> Use a comma after the *if* clause if it comes first in the sentence.
> Use *were* for the past tense of *be* with all subjects in the *if* clause.

PRACTICE 1

Use the cues to write questions and answers.

1. what / you / do / teacher / give a lot of homework / tonight
   What will you do if the teacher gives a lot of homework tonight? I'll stay up late studying.

2. you / have to cook dinner tonight / what / you / make

   _____

3. you / have free time this weekend / what / you / do

   _____

4. where / you / go / you / want to have a snack after class

   _____

5. you / want to practice English / who / you / talk to

   _____

6. what / happen / you get a good grade in this class

   _____

▪ Modals and expressions for necessity

Modal / Expression	Example	Meaning
must	You **must** take an international English exam before you study overseas.	This is necessary.
must not (mustn't)	You **must not** use a dictionary when you take the exam!	This is not allowed
have to	You **have to** get a student ID card before you register for your classes.	This is necessary.
not have to	You **don't have to** show your ID to get into the classroom.	This is not necessary.
need to	You **need to** be at the university one week before classes start.	This is necessary.
not need to	You **don't need to** be at the university three weeks before classes start.	This is not necessary.
should	You **should** study for several days before an important test.	This is a good idea.
should not (shouldn't)	You **shouldn't** stay up late the night before an important test.	This is a bad idea.

Always use the base form of the verb after modals (such as **must** and **should**).

Modals don't take **–s, –ed,** or **–ing** endings

Expressions used as modals take **–s, –ed,** or **–ing** endings (such as **have to** and **need to**).

PRACTICE 1

What are the requirements for getting a driver's license in your country? Complete the sentences with *modals* and *expressions* from the chart.

1. You _____ pass a driving test.
2. You _____ own a car.
3. You _____ take lessons at a driving school.
4. You _____ have an eye test.
5. You _____ practice driving on busy streets.
6. You _____ buy car insurance.
7. You _____ take a written test.

PRACTICE 2

Write sentences about your class and your school, using the *modals* and *expressions* given.

1. not have to *We don't have to show our notebooks to the teacher.* _____
2. should _____
3. have to _____
4. must not _____
5. need to _____
6. must _____

Unit 2

Modals and expressions for suggestions and advice

Modal / Expression	Example	Meaning
(Maybe) You should...	Maybe you **should** apply for several different kinds of jobs. You **shouldn't** be late for a job interview.	This is a good idea. This is a bad idea.
If I were you, I would/ wouldn't	**If I were you, I would/wouldn't. . .** look for work in a big company. **If I were you, I wouldn't** apply for jobs in another city.	This is what I would do in that situation.
You could...	You **could** call the company and ask if they have any job openings.	This is something you can try.
I (don't) think it's a good idea to...	**I think it's a good idea to** buy a new suit for your interview. **I don't think it's a good idea to** call the company every day!	This is my opinion of this plan.

> Use the base form of the verb after modals (such as *could, should,* and *would*).
> Modals don't take *–s, –ed,* or *–ing* endings.

PRACTICE 1

Match the sentence parts to give advice for getting a job.

1. I think it's a good idea ___
2. Maybe you should ___
3. If I were you, I ___
4. I don't think ___
5. If I were you, I wouldn't ___

a. wait too long to start job hunting.
b. would write a new resume.
c. to thank your interviewer.
d. it's a good idea to wear jeans to your interview.
e. look for jobs online.

PRACTICE 2

Your friend wants to get a job that requires English. Give suggestions and advice using the expressions.

1. could

_____

2. I think it's a good idea

_____

3. If I were you, I wouldn't

_____

4. shouldn't

_____

5. should

_____

◼ Verb + infinitive, verb + gerund

Common verbs followed by gerunds			Common verbs followed by infinitives		
enjoy	going	avoid	want	to go	need
stop	finish	quit	hope	expect	decide
appreciate	keep on	consider	promise	agree	refuse

Common verbs followed by either gerunds or infinitives (same meaning)			Common verbs followed by either gerunds or infinitives (different meanings)
like	go / to go	prefer	remember
hate	begin	start	*I remembered to pay the bill.* (= First I remembered the bill, then I paid it.)
continue	love		*I remembered paying the bill.* (= First I paid the bill. Then I remembered paying it.)
			forget
			stop
			try

PRACTICE 1

Complete the sentences. Use a verb in the *infinitive* or *gerund* form.

1. I enjoy _going to the movies on weekends._____.
2. I love _____.
3. I decided _____.
4. I hate _____.
5. I dislike _____.
6. I want _____.
7. I avoid _____.
8. I finished _____.
9. I try _____.

PRACTICE 2

Read the sentences, then answer the questions.

1. I forgot telling Jane about the party.
   Does Jane know about the party now?   Yes ____   No ____
2. Paul stopped to smoke after finishing work.
   Did Paul quit smoking?   Yes ____   No ____
3. I didn't remember to return my library books.
   Are the books at the library now?   Yes ____   No ____

◾ Unreal conditionals in the present or future

Condition   **Result**

If + subject + past tense verb	Subject + *would* + verb
If Jack had more time,	he would do volunteer work.
If I weren't so tired,	I would go to the gym after work.

Yes/no questions

If + subject + past tense verb, *would* + subject + verb?	Short answer
If Beth had time off from work, would she go away on vacation?	Yes, she would.
If you didn't have to work tonight, would you go to the party?	Yes, I would.

Wh- questions

If + subject + past tense verb, *wh*- word + *would* + subject + verb	Answer
If you wanted to find a job quickly, where would you look?	I would look online.
If you didn't have to go to class, what would you do all day?	I would sleep!

> **Unreal conditionals** talk about situations in the present or future that are not real or not possible. You don't think they will happen.
> The **if** clause can come first or second in the sentence:
>   I would go to the gym after work if I weren't so tired.
>   Where would they live if they had more money?
> Use a comma after the **if** clause if it comes first in the sentence.
> Use **were** for the past tense of **be** with all subjects in the **if** clause.

PRACTICE 1
Use the cues to write questions and answers.

1. win the lottery   *What would you do if you won the lottery? If I won the lottery, I would buy presents for all my friends.*

2. can travel anywhere _____

3. be the president of this country _____

4. teach this class _____

5. can live anywhere in the world _____

6. have a well-paying job _____

7. speak perfect English _____

Unit 3

Comparative and superlative forms of adjectives

Type of adjective	Simple form	Comparative	Superlative
one syllable	dark	darker	the darkest
one syllable ending in -e	nice	nicer	the nicest
ending in consonant + vowel + consonant	big	bigger	the biggest
ending in -y	noisy	noisier	the noisiest
two or more syllables	modern	more modern	the most modern
irregular	good	better	the best
	bad	worse	the worst
	far	farther	the farthest

Use the comparative form to compare two objects or persons.

If the second **object or person** is mentioned in the comparison, use ***than*** before it.

Use the superlative form to compare a group of objects or persons.

Use ***the*** before superlative adjectives.

PRACTICE 1

Write the comparative and superlative form of each adjective.

1. elegant _____
2. hard _____
3. intelligent _____
4. weak _____
5. lazy _____
6. difficult _____
7. useful _____
8. thin _____
9. practical _____
10. cheap _____

PRACTICE 2

Write comparisons for each pair of things and give your reasons.

1. city life / small town life / enjoyable   *Small town life is more enjoyable than city life because it's*
   more relaxed and peaceful.
2. e-mails / letters / good   _____
3. apartments / houses / convenient   _____
4. cell phones / regular phones / practical   _____
5. motorcycles / cars / dangerous   _____

PRACTICE 3

Write sentences using the *superlative* form of adjectives. Use your own ideas.

1. exciting / sport in the Olympics   *I think skiing is the most exciting sport in the Olympics*
   because the skiers go so fast.
2. beautiful / craft in our country   _____
   _____
3. good / restaurant in our town   _____
   _____
4. big / problem in the world today   _____

The passive voice

Passive voice	subject + *be* + past participle (+ by agent)
Affirmative statement	**Coffee is grown** in Brazil (by farmers). subject + *be* + past participle
Negative statement	**I was not told** about the meeting (by my boss). subject + *be* + *not* + past participle
Yes/no questions	**Is Christmas celebrated** in your country? *be* + subject + past participle
Wh- questions	**Where was that vase made?** *Wh-* word + *be* + subject + past participle

The passive voice can be used with any verb tense. Change the form of the **be** verb to indicate the tense.

Sentences in the passive voice talk mainly about the result of the action, not the person who does the action (the agent).

Include the agent in the sentence only if that information is important.

PRACTICE 1

Rewrite each sentence in the *passive voice*.

1. A French man invented Braille.

_____

2. Young people in many countries play baseball.

_____

3. Two university students started that company.

_____

4. Over one billion people speak Chinese.

_____

5. William Shakespeare wrote Hamlet.

_____

PRACTICE 2

Complete the sentence with the correct form of the verb in the *active* or *passive voice*.

1. Our homework _____ (collect) by the teacher every day.
2. Nowadays, foreign languages _____ (learn) by more and more young children.
3. Portuguese _____ (speak) in Brazil and Portugal.
4. Every year, millions of tourists _____ (visit) Mexico.
5. Wood _____ (use) in thousands of different products.
6. Banana trees _____ (find) in warm, sunny climates.
7. Dictionaries _____ (sell) at the university bookstore.
8. A man from Scotland _____ (invent) the first TV.

Unreal conditionals in the past

Condition	**Result**
If + subject + *had* + past participle	Subject + *would have* + past participle
If I had known you were in the hospital,	I would have visited you.
If they had been absent,	they wouldn't have heard about the test.
If I had told you the story,	you wouldn't have believed me.

Yes/no questions

If + subject + *had* + past participle, *would* + subject + *have* + past participle
If you had applied to graduate school, would you have been accepted?
If you had heard about the party, would you have gone to it?
If they had started studying earlier, would they have passed the test?

***Wh-* questions**

If + subject + *had* + past participle, *wh-* word + *would* + subject + *have* + past participle
If you had needed help, who would you have asked?
If you had known about the problem, what would you have done?
If there had been a fire, how would you have gotten out of the building?

> Unreal conditionals in the past talk about situations in the past that were not real or not possible.
> The *if* clause can come first or second in the sentence:
>
> You wouldn't have believed me if I had told you that story.
> Would you have been accepted if you had applied to graduate school?
> Who would you have asked if you had needed help?
>
> Use a comma after the *if* clause if it comes first in the sentence.

PRACTICE 1

How would your life have been different in these unreal situations? Write sentences with your own ideas.

1. you were born male/female _____*If I had been born*_____

   _____

2. you lived one hundred years ago _____

   _____

3. you were born in Australia _____

   _____

4. you went to a different high school _____

   _____

5. you had different parents _____

   _____

6. (your own idea) _____

   _____

Unit 4

Perfect modals for speculating about the past

Perfect modal	Example	Use
might have	French people in the Middle Ages **might have** had many health problems, because they didn't take baths.	making a guess
must have	People **must have** had very bad teeth, because they didn't have toothbrushes.	saying you're sure about something
could have	People **could have** used plants from their gardens as medicine.	saying something is possible
couldn't have	People **couldn't have** known about bacteria, because they didn't have microscopes.	saying something is not possible

Use perfect modals with the past participle form of the verb.

Remember that modals don't take *–s, –ed,* or *–ing* endings.

PRACTICE 1

Write three sentences for each situation, using different *perfect modals* in each sentence.

1. Glenn got 38% on his math test.

    a. _____

    b. _____

    c. _____

2. Sara is reading an e-mail and she has a big smile on her face.

    a. _____

    b. _____

    c. _____

3. Our teacher never misses class, but he wasn't here today.

    a. _____

    b. _____

    c. _____

4. Mark looks really tired this morning.

    a. _____

    b. _____

    c. _____

5. Liliana always comes to work on time, but today she was an hour late.

    a. _____

    b. _____

    c. _____

Past continuous vs. simple past

Past perfect	subject + *was/were* + present participle
Affirmative statement	**I was watching** TV at 10:00 last night. subject + *was/were* + present participle
Negative statement	**I was not studying** at 10:00. subject + *was/were* + not + present participle
Yes/no questions	**Were you sleeping** at 10:00? *was/were* + subject + present participle
Wh- questions	**What were you doing** at 10:00? *Wh-* word + *was/ were* + subject + present participle

Use the past continuous:
- to talk about actions that were already in progress at a given time in the past.
- together with the simple past to show that one action began and was in progress when another action happened.

PRACTICE 1

Write answers with the *past continuous*.

1. What were you doing last night at 10:00?
   Last night at 10:00, _____.

2. What were you doing in 2003?
   _____.

3. What were you doing on Saturday afternoon?
   _____.

4. What were you doing the last time your phone rang?
   _____.

PRACTICE 2

Write sentences about two events using the *simple past* and *past continuous*.
Use *when* or *while*.

1. brother / come home / I / watch TV
   My brother came home while I was watching TV. _____

2. I / take a bath / doorbell / ring
   _____

3. we / go to school / it / start raining
   _____

4. she / run to the bus stop / she / fall
   _____

5. our teacher / work / we / go into his office
   _____

6. Linda / walk on the beach / she / find a necklace
   _____

Past perfect vs. simple past

Past perfect	subject + *had* + past participle
Affirmative statement	**I had cooked dinner** when the guests arrived. subject + *had* + past participle
Negative statement	**I had not cleaned** the kitchen when they arrived. subject + *had* + *not* + past participle
Yes/no questions	**Had you seen** that man before last night? *had* + subject + past participle
Wh- questions	**Where had you seen** him before? *Wh-* word + *had* + subject + past participle

Use the past perfect:
- to talk about actions that were completed before another action or time in the past.
- together with the simple past to show when two actions happened.
- for the earlier action, and the simple past for the later action.

In sentences with **before** or **after,** you don't need the past perfect because the time relationship is already expressed.

PRACTICE 1
Read the sentences and circle the correct verb forms. There may be more than one correct answer.

1. The fire (started / had started) because somebody (forgot / had forgotten) to turn off the stove.
2. The volunteers (made / had made) a presentation about the house after they (finished / had finished) making the displays.
3. The movie (began / had begun) when I (got / had gotten) to the theater, so I (sat / had sat) in the back.
4. I (was / had been) very hungry at noon because I (didn't eat / hadn't eaten) breakfast.
5. Jason (graduated / had graduated) from the university before he (got / had gotten) married.

PRACTICE 2
Write one sentence with *because* about each pair of events, using the *past perfect* and *simple past.*

1. My eyes were red. I studied for six hours.

_____

2. Lisa was excited. She found a job.

_____

3. I ran ten kilometers. My legs were tired.

_____

4. I practiced for two months. The driving test was easy.

_____

Unit 5

Simple present and present continuous for future

Simple present (base form of verb + -s with *he, she, it*)
Use the simple present to express future time when talking about fixed schedules, timetables, and programs.
Present continuous (*be* + present participle)
Use the present continuous to talk about future plans and arrangements that have already been made.

PRACTICE 1

Check ✓ the sentences that refer to future time.

_____ 1. The final exam in this class is in December.
_____ 2. Fred is having dinner with his grandparents on Friday night.
_____ 3. I read the newspaper every morning on the train.
_____ 4. Why are you laughing at me?
_____ 5. My sister arrives on Wednesday.
_____ 6. Tom speaks Spanish, but not very well
_____ 7. Where are you going over the holidays?
_____ 8. I'm trying to study! Please turn off the TV.
_____ 9. The next bus leaves at 3:30.
_____ 10. Sarah doesn't drive a car very often.

PRACTICE 2

A classmate wants to have coffee with you, but you don't want to. Make excuses by talking about your plans for these times.

1. after class today
   I'm sorry, I _____

2. this evening
   _____

3. tomorrow night
   _____

4. Saturday afternoon
   _____

5. next Tuesday
   _____

PRACTICE 3

Complete the sentences with the correct form of the verb in the *simple present* or *present continuous.*

1. What _____ (you, do) tomorrow?
2. On Saturday, _____ (we, go) to a concert in the park.
3. The concert _____ (start) at 8 p.m.
4. I heard that you _____ (move) to New York next month!
5. We _____ (have) lunch in the cafeteria after class.
   _____ (you, come) with us?
6. What time _____ (the plane, arrive)?
7. You have ten minutes to finish the test. It _____ (end) at 2:00.

▪ *Will* to express future time

Will	subject + *will* + base form
Affirmative statement	**I will call you** tomorrow. subject + *will* + base form
Negative statement	**I won't be** home tomorrow. subject + *will* + *not* + base form
Yes/no questions	**Will you have** time to see me? *will* + subject + base form
Wh- questions	**What will you do** if you don't find your keys? *Wh-* word + *will* + subject + base form

Use *will*:
- to make a quick decision
- to make a serious promise
- to make a prediction

PRACTICE 1

What will these things be like in your city twenty years in the future? Write predictions.

1. transportation _____

2. shopping _____

3. schools _____

4. housing _____

5. the environment _____

PRACTICE 2

Make promises for these situations.

1. Your boss says, "You come to work five minutes late every day!"

2. Your English teacher says, "I can't read your handwriting!"

3. Your grandmother says, "You never come to visit me!"

4. Your doctor says, "You need to get more exercise!"

5. Your parents say, "You never listen to our advice!"

■ *Going to*

Going to	subject + *be* + *going to* + base form
Affirmative statement	**I am going to take** a vacation next month. subject + *be* + *going to* + base form
Negative statement	**I'm not going to buy** a car. subject + *be* + not + *going to* + base form
Yes/no questions	**Are you going to look** for a job? *be* + subject + *going to* + base form
Wh- questions	**Where are you going to look** for a job? *Wh-* word + *be* + subject + *going to* + base form

Use *going to*:
- to talk about intentions for the future
- to talk about something that will happen very soon or immediately
- to make a simple prediction

PRACTICE 1
Unscramble the sentences.

1. are / when / finish / you / to / your / going / homework

   _____

2. tonight / going / I / am / TV / to / watch

   _____

3. we / are / to / have / next Saturday / going / a party

   _____

4. you / are / going / cook / dinner / what / for / to

   _____

5. am / tomorrow / not / going / go / I / shopping / to

   _____

6. new / buy / Cathy / is / to / a / computer / going

   _____

PRACTICE 2
Write sentences about your future intentions for these times.

1. tonight _____
2. tomorrow _____
3. this weekend _____
4. next week _____
5. next vacation _____

Indirect questions

Direct question	Polite phrase	Indirect question
Where is the office?	Do you know	**where** the office is?
When does the interview start?	Can you tell me	**when** the interview starts?
Is she a sociologist?	I was wondering	**whether/if** she's a sociologist.

An indirect question is a question that's placed inside another question or statement. Indirect questions are used in more formal, polite speech.

In an indirect **wh- question,** the subject comes before the verb in the question.

In an indirect **yes/no question,** use **whether** (more formal) or **if** (less formal) in the question.

Don't use the auxiliary **do/does** in indirect questions.

PRACTICE 1

Make these questions more polite by rewriting them as *embedded questions.*

1. Where's the ticket machine?

   _____

2. What time does the flight to Caracas leave?

   _____

3. Is there a telephone near here?

   _____

4. When will Professor Adams be back?

   _____

5. Does this bus go to Capitol Square?

   _____

6. Who is that man in the gray suit?

   _____

PRACTICE 2

Read the ad and write polite *indirect questions* about the information.

Improve your English at Academy Language Institute! We have the most modern methods and highly-trained teachers. Convenient class times from early morning to late night, with special weekend courses available. Register today for next month's classes.

1. _____
   They cost $60 a month.

2. _____
   Our teachers are from Canada and Australia, and also from this country.

3. _____
   The first class starts at 6:30 a.m.

4. _____
   Yes, we do. We have business English classes in the evening.

5. _____
   No, I'm sorry. You have to come to the school to register.

Vocabulary for the Humanities

Philosophy terms

Term	Definition	Sentence
aesthetics	the branch of philosophy that focuses on the nature of beauty and art	A good aesthetic sense helps you distinguish between music that is beautiful and pleasing to hear and that which is just a noisy combination of sounds.
analogy	a kind of logic when you reason that if two things are similar in some ways they are in other ways too	In an analogy, a seedling is to a plant as a child is to an adult because both have the potential to grow to their mature state.
ancients and moderns	a philosophical argument about whether the authority of ancient learning is more or less important than one's current ability to think about problems	The debate between ancients and moderns sometimes becomes a conflict between religion and science.
being	the state of existing or someone's basic nature	Nuclear weapons threaten my very being.
civil disobedience	a peaceful resistance to law by non-cooperation	Mahatma Gandhi used civil disobedience to drive the British Empire out of India.
classification	putting items in groups according to type	Modern biological classification includes two major types of fish with jaws: those with bones and those without bones.
cosmology	the study of the nature of the universe as a whole	Astronomers who are interested in cosmology have found that the universe is expanding rapidly.
criticism	judging the artistic qualities of something	Literary criticism looks at both the good and bad points of literature.
cycles	the idea that things take place in a sequence of events that gets repeated	Some philosophers believe that art styles go in cycles between very classical or understated forms and very expressive or extreme ones.
democracy	government based on the free participation of everyone who is governed	In a democracy everyone is entitled to vote for their next leader.
determinism	the idea that everything including human behavior is caused by something, and that there really is no such thing as free will.	People who believe in geographic determinism think that your physical surroundings determine how successful your country will be.
duality	having two opposing sides or parts in equal measure	Physicists may treat waves and particles as a duality just as philosophers may treat body and mind as a duality.
empirical	knowledge obtained through the senses	We do empirical research when we examine nature directly with our hands, eyes and instruments.
Enlightenment	an intellectual movement in the 18th century (1700s) that emphasized science and reason	During the Enlightenment, reason was more important than faith or empirical studies for understanding the natural world.
entropy	part of the second law of thermodynamics that measures disorder in a system to see how close it is to equilibrium or balance	The human race is in a perpetual state of entropy.
epistemology	the study of the origins and limits of knowledge	Epistemologists analyze the ultimate sources of knowledge including divine revelation, reasoning by means of logic and mathematics, and observation and experimentation in the sciences.
ethics	the branch of philosophy that deals with morality and human behavior	Mr. King is a very successful businessman, but his employees often question his ethics when he takes advantage of customers.
evolution	the process by which species change slowly or quickly as a result of genetic mutation and natural selection	We can see early traces of the evolution of life on earth from about four billion years ago.
free will	the power to make your own choices in life	Bob believes in free will because he thinks he can choose what will happen in his life.
hierarchy	a group whose members are organized in ranks based on differences in wealth, power, importance, etc.	The highest person in a hierarchy may be the Pope, the President or the Chief Executive Officer, depending upon the hierarchy to which they belong.

Term	Definition	Sentence
humanism	a movement that emphasized the needs of people instead of religious ideas	Advocates of humanism are more concerned with saving lives than with saving souls, so they are more likely to provide medical care than to work as preachers
iconoclast	a person who challenges or rejects traditional beliefs	A great philosopher must be a traditionalist who respects the work of his predecessors as well as an iconoclast who rejects it.
infinity	a limitless number, thing, or place such as outer space or time	We cannot imagine the end of time so we think of time as infinite or having no end.
justice	validity in the law and fairness in applying it	Court systems provide justice to people involved in disputes and crimes.
macrocosm	a large, complicated system that is seen as a single unit	We can study the ecology of a desert island as one thing, but really it is a macrocosm of many different systems.
metaphor	a figure of speech which suggests similarity between one thing and another	"All that glitters is not gold" is a metaphor for saying that things aren't always what they seem to be.
metaphysics	the branch of philosophy that deals with the nature of reality and knowledge	Metaphysical discussions often ask whether what we think is real is experienced the same way by everyone.
microcosm	a small version of a much larger thing	Our class is a microcosm of the whole university in its composition.
philosophy	the study of the most general truths and beliefs about the nature and meaning of humankind, the world, and the conduct of life; word from Greek meaning "the love of wisdom"	My friends and I have late night discussions about philosophy because we're trying to make sense of our lives and our place in the world.
positivism	a theory of knowledge based on observation	Positivism supports experimentation but has little interest in mystical experiences.
pragmatism	a philosophical movement that believed that all theories need to be tested in real life	Pragmatists believe that an idea must be tried in real life instead of just assuming that something is true in an absolute sense.
rationalism	a theory that knowledge is based on principles called axioms and that you can logically arrive at understanding by reasoning	My friend Don is a rationalist because he believes that you can reason your way to understanding everything.
structuralism	the view of society as a system or network with interconnecting parts that can be analyzed to understand how the whole works	Some structuralists look at society as a kind of machine with parts that all work together.
uniformity	a belief that the same natural laws apply throughout the universe	People who believe in uniformity in the 21st century probably would have believed in a universe based on perfect circles six hundred years ago.
utopia	a place of ideal peace, cooperation and good living	Throughout history, people have tried to create utopian communities, but they never seem to succeed.

Language terms

Term	Definition	Sentence
acquisition	the process of learning a new language in a natural way as a young child would	By living with a family for a year, Laura experienced natural acquisition of Portuguese instead of learning it though classes and textbooks.
affixes	morphemes added to a word that change its meaning or function	Adding the affix "un" to the root "kind" reverses its meaning and adding "ly" changes its function.
alphabet	a writing system that uses letters to represent certain sounds	The Cyrillic alphabet represents sounds in the Russian and Slavic languages.
bilingual	someone who speaks two languages fluently	Sophia is fluently bilingual in Romanian and Italian although she knows about six other languages less well.
borrowing	the movement of a word from one language to another	When a word is borrowed from another language it is called a "loan word" at first.
cliché	a word or expression that has been overused so it has lost its meaning	If you describe someone by saying they are "nice" it really doesn't mean much because the word has become a cliché.

Term	Definition	Sentence
code switching	when a speaker changes between several dialects or languages in a single conversation.	As I listened to his telephone conversation, Abdulkarim effortlessly code switched between Berber, French, Arabic and English.
collocation	words that commonly or frequently occur together such as phrasal verbs or idioms	"Lived happily ever after" is a collocation used to end fairy tales.
corpus linguistics	the empirical study of large collections of actual speech and writing (corpora) to determine how people actually use language	The lexicial approach is based on what linguists have learned from corpus linguistics
dialect	a language variety where the use of vocabulary, grammar, and pronunciation is specific to a geographic region or social class	People from the Appalachian Mountains speak with a dialect that is distinctive in vocabulary, grammar and pronunciation.
discourse	the use of larger units of language (paragraphs, conversations, essays) in communication	Kaplan noted that people in different cultures have different discourse styles when they present an argument.
endangered language	languages that are dying out because they have few native speakers	At one point, Gaelic was an endangered language, but it has made a comeback.
etymology	the study of word origins and history	Words change meaning over time, thus etymology shows us that a word like "awesome" has a very different sense now than it did 400 years ago.
hieroglyphics	a writing system where pictures represent objects, ideas, or sound	Ancient Egyptians used hieroglyphics for record-keeping over 5,000 years ago.
idiom	a fixed expression where the actual meaning differs from the literal meaning of the phrase	"It is raining buckets" doesn't mean that water pails are falling from the sky, but that it is raining very heavily.
interpretation	a change from one language to another taking into account the nature of each language so that the meaning remains the same	Our interpreter was equally familiar with our language and that of our hosts, so she was careful to make sure each statement was expressed fully and not just given a rough translation.
language	learned human communication by systems of written symbols, spoken words, and movements	Some animals have very sophisticated communication systems, but scientists think that true language is specific to human beings.
language families	a classification system of the world's languages into related families that share a common ancestor and have many features in common	Celtic languages are part of the Indo-European language family and include Welsh, Gaelic, Manx, Breton, and Cornish.
lexicon	the set of all the words and idioms used in a language	A dictionary contains the lexicon or vocabulary of a language.
linguist	a person who studies languages, their structure and history	Jill is a linguist who knows 16 languages and understands how they are related.
native speaker	a person who naturally acquires a language as a young child and therefore has an intuitive understanding of how it works	Native speakers often have problems giving grammar rules because they have never learned them as rules, but simply internalized them and used them.
neurolinguistics	the part of linguistics that studies how the human brain processes language	Neurolinguistics has shown that repetition and use are important when we learn new vocabulary items.
phonetics	the scientific study of the sound system of a language	Linguists use phonetics to record the sounds of unwritten languages.
pictograph	a writing system where a picture represents a word or idea	In the Japanese *kanji* writing system, pictographs or characters represent ideas.
pragmatics	the part of linguistic study that focuses on language in actual use instead of on structure	Deborah Tannen has recently published research on the pragmatics of conversations between mothers and daughters.
prescriptivism	the assertion that there is a "best" or "correct" form of a language	Prescriptivism discriminates against minority groups and immigrants who have their own legitimate forms of language.
register	language that is appropriate to communication with a particular social group	You wouldn't use the same register to make a request from your roommate and your professor.
roots	the basic part of a word that has meaning by itself, to which affixes can be added	In the word "kindness," "kind" is the root, meaning *generous* or *caring*.

Term	Definition	Sentence
RP	received pronunciation or a BBC model of British English	Sometimes employers insist that their staff speak RP in public settings.
semantics	the study of meaning in language through words, symbols, and sentences	Since people assign quite different meanings to the same words, a lot of disagreement can occur in a semantic discussion.
sign language	a system of hand signs used for communication by people with severe hearing disabilities	Jane originally learned sign language so she could communicate with her deaf sister, but later she found that it was a very useful skill as a social worker.
sociolinguistics	the study of the relationship between language, society, and culture	Sociolinguistics helps us to understand how people who live in the same area use different forms of the same language in pronunciation, vocabulary, and grammar.
syntax	the organization or grammar of words at the sentence level	Although English is a Germanic language, the syntax is very different from German.
translation	to change something from one language to another	Although the conference speaker's paper was in Hungarian, it was translated into eight other languages.

Art terms

Term	Definition	Sentence
abstract art	an art style from the 20th century that was more concerned with shape than with objects or people that you could recognize	Jackson Pollock's abstract paintings were often made by dripping or pouring paint onto a canvas in random order.
architecture	the art and science of making buildings	Some of the wonders of modern architecture are the skyscrapers of Malaysia and Taiwan.
Art Nouveau	an artistic style popular in the 1800s which featured many curved shapes and lines	Some of the Paris subway stops are decorated in Art Nouveau style with signs and ironwork that look like leaves and flowers.
arts and crafts	traditional items created by hand; sometimes the artist is known, but often not; similar or identical items created for practical use	The local arts and crafts shop features baskets, quilts, and weaving done in the traditional style of this region.
Baroque	European artistic style from the 1600s that was very ornate or highly decorated	There are many fine examples of Baroque architecture in Latin America because that was the most popular style at the time in Spain and Portugal.
bas relief	a kind of sculpture where the raised part is attached to a flat surface	Blind people enjoy touching the bas relief panels on the wall because they can feel the raised pictures.
calligraphy	handwriting letters in an artistic way	Arabic calligraphy requires a great deal of skill to form the letters precisely, but the results are beautiful.
carving	making sculpture by cutting away the unwanted parts	Gilbert likes to carve big statues of bears out of wood.
casting	making sculpture by using a mold	You have to prepare the mold first when you cast a piece of sculpture.
ceramics	another general term for pottery	Archaeologists often use broken pieces of ceramics to tell how old a site is.
chiseling	like carving, but done with a tool called a chisel	Indians on the Northwest Coast chiseled huge totem poles out of tall trees.
decorative arts	useful arts intended for use in the home or by people such as furniture, jewelry, clothing	Cindy is a very talented designer of decorative arts with her own jewelry studio.
drawing	a picture drawn with pen, pencil, or crayon, often black and white	Some painters make a quick drawing or sketch before they start to paint.
engraving	a picture or design cut or etched into a hard surface that later can be used for printing	Sailors used to make detailed engravings called scrimshaw on pieces of bone during their long weeks at sea.
Expressionism	a twentieth century art style which focused on feelings to the extent that images were often distorted	You can almost hear the person scream in Edvard Munch's expressionist painting.

Term	Definition	Sentence
fine arts	unique art items created by known artists with formal training	The fine arts museum has priceless paintings and sculpture by famous artists.
folk art	another term for arts and crafts	Mexican folk art such as embroidery and pottery is very colorful.
fresco	a painting done with watercolors on walls or ceilings while the plaster is still wet	That old castle in Italy had frescoes painted on every wall.
gallery	a place where an artist shows his/her work, often for sale	Let's go to the new exhibit of paintings that's opening at the gallery tonight.
glaze	a shiny finish or coating that is put on pottery to make it waterproof	Chinese pottery often has blue painting done over a white glaze.
graphic arts	art that depends more on line than color (drawing, printing, calligraphy)	Some graphic arts students prefer abstract printing, but Tanya likes to design clothing.
Impressionism	a popular art and music style in France in the late 1800s and early 1900s which created a mood or impression, often of a landscape	Jim's favorite impressionist work is Monet's paintings of water lilies in his garden.
kiln	an oven in which pottery is baked at high temperatures	Ella had to wait three hours for the kiln to cool down before she could open it.
landscape	a painting or drawing of beautiful scenery in the countryside	The English painter Turner is famous for landscapes of the countryside in stormy weather.
linear perspective	the technique of making images seem closer or more distant; creating an illusion of three dimensions in a medium that only uses two, such as painting or drawing	If you look at old paintings before linear perspective was invented, everything seems to be crowded into the front of the painting.
model	1. a small version of a large building that architects use in the process of design; 2. a person who poses for an artist	The architects made small models of the proposed building to show what it would look like when it was finished.
mosaic	a picture made from thousands of tiny pieces of glass or tile	That Roman mosaic picture must have 10,000 pieces of glass in it.
mural	a very large painting on walls	The students painted a mural on the side of the arts building to show scenes from history.
oil	painting using pigments mixed with oil	You can paint over your mistakes with oil colors, but the paints sure have a strong smell!
optical illusion	a visual experience that fools the eye into seeing something that is not really there	The Dutch artist M. C. Esher is famous for his optical illusions that made shapes change into other shapes and stairs go up and down at the same time.
painting	art that is made by using a brush or some other tool to put paint onto flat surfaces.	Most people do painting with a brush, but some people use spray cans to paint graffiti.
photography	art done with a camera	Ansel Adams' famous photography of landscapes was mostly done in black and white.
pigment	natural or artificial materials that give paint or ink its color	If you grind up this red rock, you can use it as pigment with some water.
plastic arts	art with three dimensions such as sculpture, pottery or architecture	Think of plastic art as something that you can shape with your hands.
portrait	a picture of a person	You have to sit very still for a long time if some is going to paint your portrait.
pottery	artistic objects made by shaping moist clay and later baking it in a hot kiln	Japanese pottery called *raku* has been made in the same way for hundreds of years.
primary colors	three basic colors (magenta, yellow and cyan) from which all other colors can be made	Michael's paintings usually use just the primary colors of red, blue, and yellow.
print-making	art made by pressing an inked raised surface on paper	The good thing about print-making is that you can make several copies of your work from the same carving.

Term	Definition	Sentence
Renaissance	the European artistic style that followed Gothic in the 1500s with many influences from ancient Greece and Rome	Leonardo da Vinci and Michelangelo are among the most famous artists of the Renaissance.
Romantic	The main artistic style of the 1700s which emphasized emotion and nature	Romantic art is very dramatic and emotional in contrast to earlier classical art styles.
sculpture	three dimensional art created by sculpting, modeling, or casting	Some modern artists make sculptures out of used automobile parts.
self-portrait	a picture an artist draws of himself or herself	The Mexican artist Frida Kahlo painted many self-portraits at different times in her life.
stained glass	glass that has been colored and put together to form a picture in a window, often in a church or cathedral	The sunlight coming through the stained glass made a lovely pattern of light on the floor.
still life	a picture of something that is not living such as fruit, flowers, or food, usually done in a home setting	The Dutch artist Vermeer did still-life paintings of things he saw around his house such as dishes and food.
studio	a workshop where an artist produces art	Tim's studio is a bit of a mess with unfinished paintings all over the place.
tempera	painting using pigments mixed with water and egg	The ancient wall paintings in Egypt were done with tempera paints and egg.
watercolor	a type of painting that uses pigments that are mixed with water and applied to a wet surface	My uncle loves to paint watercolors, but he has to work very fast before the paper dries out.

History terms

Term	Definition	Sentence
absolute dating	assigning dates to things using known measurements such as carbon 14 or the number of tree rings	Absolute dating using radiocarbon shows that farmers grew corn in the Tehuacan Valley 4500 years ago.
antiquity	ancient history, especially referring to Greek and Roman times	Democracy started in antiquity when the word meant "rule of the people" in Greek.
B.C. and A.D.	markers in Western history using the birth of Christ as a turning point. Events B.C. are before that point and events A.D. are after that point two millennia ago	The Roman Empire dates from 27 B.C. to 395 A.D.
census data	Most governments count their people every ten or more years and historians use information from these reports	You can see changes in a population if you look at the census data every ten years for a century.
century	one hundred years; "-th century" refers to the previous 100 years	The Mughal Empire flourished in India during the 1700s or the eighteenth century.
chronology	a list or description of events in the order in which they happen	Peter understands the events that led up to the French Revolution because he made a chronology.
civilization	a highly developed society with central organization, cities, and the use of writing	The first civilizations occurred in Mesopotamia, the area between the Tigris and Euphrates Rivers in the Middle East.
colonialism	a system in which one country rules other countries and takes things from them to benefit the ruling country	Social scientists believe that you can blame colonialism for many of the social problems in the world today.
conquest	a military victory	Military conquest does not mean that people will be loyal to the new rulers.
decade	ten years	The drought lasted for three decades and people were overjoyed when rains returned after 30 years.
document	a piece of writing that gives information about the past	Someday your grocery list may become an interesting historical document.
dynasty	a series of people from one family who rule a country	The Han Dynasty (206 B.C. to 220 A.D.) was the golden age of Chinese philosophy, which saw the rise of both Confucianism and Buddhism.
emigration	when people leave their country to go live in another country	The population of Sweden declined due to emigration to America.

Term	Definition	Sentence
empire	a group of nations ruled by a central government usually led by an emperor	The Mongol Empire started by Genghis Khan was the largest land empire in history.
epidemic	a disease that spreads quickly among many people	During the Middle Ages, the plague epidemic spread throughout Europe.
era	a time period with certain characteristics	The Victorian era, during the reign of Queen Victoria in England, was a time of conservative attitudes.
excavation	the careful technique that archaeologists use to dig a site	As the excavation proceeded, the archaeologists mapped everything they found.
feudalism	the most common political system in medieval times when the king and the upper classes owned the land and the lower classes worked it and served in the military.	Feudalism is best known from medieval Europe, but it also happened in Africa, China and Japan.
frontier	the outer edge of land exploration	In the American West, settlers found native people living on the frontier.
historical archaeology	archaeology that uses written records or deals with civilizations that had writing	Historical archaeologists use both excavation of material remains (houses and forts) as well as written records to understand medieval France
history	the study of past events, people and civilizations	Santayana said that people who don't understand their history are doomed to repeat it.
immigration	the arrival of people from another country who plan to settle permanently in the new country	Immigration of people without skills from poor countries is a major political problem for receiving countries.
invasion	the 18th century change to using machines instead of human and animal power which created huge changes in society	The Viking invasions of Britain in the Middle Ages had a great influence on the English language.
medieval	referring to the Middle Ages, the time between antiquity and the Renaissance in Europe; the term is also used for Japan	Two of the greatest medieval leaders, Charlemagne and Harun ar Rashid, met and gave each other gifts around 800 A.D.
monarchy	a government run by a king, queen or other ruler by birth	The Netherlands and Nepal are both monarchies.
multilateral	many-sided or involving many countries	The Kyoto Protocol was a multilateral agreement by 160 countries to reduce greenhouse gases to improve the environment.
nationalism	a desire by people who have a common background to have their own independent country	Nationalism was one of the great historical movements of Europe in the 1800s.
pre-industrial	societies that used human and animal power to farm and produce goods; trade and exchanges were conducted without capital	The Silk Road across Asia was one of the major routes for goods and people to travel between pre-industrial societies.
primary source	original piece of writing about an event or personal experience	Memoirs, letters, and legal documents are all primary sources.
reign	the time period when a king or queen rules a country	A great deal of exploration occurred during the reign of Elizabeth I of England.
relative dating	assigning dates to something by knowing that it was earlier or later than something else	Historians use relative dating for the volcanic eruption that destroyed Santorini about 1640 B.C. using Minoan records from the nearby island of Crete.
Renaissance	the European historical period from the 14th through 17th centuries when classical ideas and art became popular again and when modern science began	During the Renaissance, scholars became interested in learning about ideas from antiquity that had been ignored during the Middle Ages.
reunification	when countries that have been apart come together again	With the reunification of Germany, many families who had been confined to East Germany were able to visit their relatives in West Germany again.
revolt	to fight against the government or other power	The peasants revolted against the king when he required them to pay new taxes.
secondary source	writing by another person about information from a primary source	Secondary sources about the Song Dynasty a thousand years ago in China use primary sources such as Li Qingzhao's diary about her daily life.

Term	Definition	Sentence
site	a place where something is, was, or happened	The archaeologists are digging at the site of an ancient Mayan temple.
slavery	a condition when people are owned by other people and get no money in return for their work	During the period of slavery many children were bought and sold and taken by their new owners far from their families.
timeline	a graphic organizer similar to a chronology with events occurring longest ago at one end of the line and most recent events at the other	Our history classroom has a timeline along the wall so we can see how events fit together.
treaty	an agreement or accord between nations	The nations of Southeast Asia signed an economic trade treaty.
xenophobia	a fear or dislike of foreigners or foreign culture	Teaching about different cultures in the schools helps to reduce xenophobia.

Social Science terms

Term	Definition	Sentence
aboriginals	the native people who first lived in a place	Aboriginal Australians say the land should be returned to them because it always was theirs before the settlers arrived.
case study	a careful analysis of one particular situation that can be used to understand similar situations	That's a famous case study of what can happen to a small island in a short period of time if people don't take care of the environment.
consumption	using goods and services as a consumer	Consumption of fizzy drinks is up 67% among students aged fifteen to eighteen.
culture	a broad term that includes human language, beliefs, values, behaviors and material things that continue from one generation to the next	Gaelic culture in Scotland almost died out before people started using the language and doing things in traditional ways again.
development	social change that shows some kind of progress	Economic aid has helped the country's development of a new telephone system.
economics	the social science concerned with how people use goods and services	Economics helps us to understand why consumers have confidence at some times and are worried about investing their money at other times.
ethnicity	belonging to a group that shares particular characteristics such as race, country or religion	The ethnicity of most of the miners was Eastern European, but a few were French.
ethnocentrism	judging other cultures by your own which you believe is better	Ethnocentric people believe that their own culture is superior, so they aren't really interested in learning about other cultures.
ethnography	a written description of the lifestyle of an ethnic group	Evans-Pritchard's ethnography of the Nuer tells about every aspect of their lives.
evolution	the gradual change of forms or political systems	The evolution of the new language was so gradual that no one noticed it.
gender roles	behaviors that are considered appropriate for males and females in a particular culture	A huge change in gender roles in recent years means that fathers feel comfortable staying home to take care of their young children.
globalization	the spread of certain forms of capitalism throughout the world	Fast food restaurants are a good example of globalization of our economy.
interview	a meeting in which a researcher asks questions	Margot held interviews with 450 people to find out how they felt about noise from the new airport.
kinship	relationships by birth, adoption, or marriage	This kinship chart shows that families from the two villages share the same ancestors and frequently intermarried.
migration	moving from one area to another; can be forced (as in the case of slavery) or voluntary	Rural to urban migration has caused a huge homeless population in the cities.
nuclear family	a husband, wife, and their children	My nuclear family consists of my parents, my brothers, my sister, and me.
political science	the social science that studies how people use and react to power through politics and government	Martin is studying political science because he wants to become a politician and work in the government.
qualitative	information from personal opinions, feelings, or judgments	This new sociological study is based on qualitative information from many interviews and questionnaires.

Term	Definition	Sentence
quantitative	information that can be measured mathematically	Pete used a computer networking program to process the quantitative data for his Ph.D. research in political science.
social institutions	the way a society organizes itself to meet basic human needs; examples are religion, education, politics, economics	Sometimes social institutions differ in their aims. The educational system wants to keep young people in school, but the military wants them to leave to join the army.
socialization	the way children learn the "rules" of their own culture and how to function within it	Schools help with socialization by setting strong expectations for student behavior.
socioeconomic status	the place or rank that you have according to your wealth, power and prestige	Most national leaders come from families with high socioeconomic status, but sometimes a leader rises out of poverty.
sociology	the social science that focuses on modern, urbanized societies and looks for universal patterns of human behavior	As part of their sociology course, the students conducted surveys to find out why people were moving to the suburbs from the city.
stereotype	ideas about what people are really like that may be true or false	It's a stereotype to think that all blondes are dumb.
stratification	the idea that classes in society form layers with different access to resources	The subsistence farmers depend on growing just enough food to feed their families.
survey	a poll or questions that have been asked of a population in order to determine their opinions	Our class did a survey to find out which students would take the bus to college instead of drive.
sustainability	change that can continue without ill effects to people or the environment	If you want tourism to last for years, you have to consider sustainability of the natural beauty of the island that attracts people.
tribal	a form of social organization where members of the group have common ancestors, customs and beliefs and leadership	The tribal council met to discuss how they should use the government's money for education.
urban	people who live in large town or city	The urban area extends from one city to the neighboring city.

 **Audio Script**

Unit 1 Lesson 1

Exercise A

CD T-1

Sandra: Hi! You must be the new exchange student.

Rafael: Yeah. I'm Rafael Moreno.

Sandra: Nice to meet you, Rafael. I'm Sandra Kelly. You're from Mexico?

Rafael: No, actually, I'm Venezuelan. I'm from Caracas.

Sandra: Your English is really good! Have you lived in this country before?

Rafael: No, I haven't. But I've studied English for eight years.

Sandra: So, are you an English major?

Rafael: Actually, I'm a philosophy major.

Sandra: Really? So, are you going to be, uhh, a philosopher after you graduate?

Rafael: No, probably not . . . My family has a shipping business, and I'm going to work for my father. But studying philosophy is useful for all kinds of things.

Sandra: It is? Like what?

Rafael: Well, for one thing, you learn how to think clearly. And you learn how to solve complicated problems.

Sandra: I guess you need that in business.

Rafael: Oh, you do. I've worked in my dad's office every summer, and there are always plenty of problems to solve!

Sandra: So, how do you like Southland so far?

Rafael: It's great, but the campus is so big . . . By the way, can you tell me where the Student Services building is? I have to go there to get my student ID card.

Sandra: Sure. I'm going over that way now — I can show you.

Rafael: Thanks so much!

Unit 1, Lesson 1

Exercise D

CD T-3

Rafael: I have obtained a student ID card. I got it on Tuesday.

I haven't met with my advisor yet, but I have made an appointment.

I've filled out a lot of forms with information about my health.

Unit 1, Lesson 2

Exercise E

CD T-4
Lecture Part I

Female professor: Good morning, everyone. This is Philosophy 420, Business Ethics — you're all in the right place? Good. First, I'd like to introduce myself. My name is Anne Wolinsky, and I'm your instructor for the course. My office is room 822 in the Humanities Building. My office hours are from 3–4:00 every afternoon, but if you need to talk to me at another time, please make an appointment with me. The textbook we'll be using in this course is *Business Ethics for Today*, and the university bookstore has plenty of copies.

Unit 1, Lesson 2

Exercise F

CD T-5
Lecture Part II

Female professor: Now, first of all, what does "business ethics" mean? And why do we study business ethics? As you all know, ethics — and business ethics — is a branch of philosophy. The English word philosophy comes from the Greek words for "love" and "wisdom." For the ancient Greeks, *philosophy* was the love of wisdom. But we need to be more specific to understand what philosophers do today.

We can say that philosophy is an area of inquiry. In it, we try to discover truths about the world — a kind of research. In some ways, philosophy is similar to science, journalism, and detective work. All of these things try to find out what is true. But philosophy is different, because the questions it asks are more general, and more important. It asks questions about God, knowledge, the mind, and what's right and wrong. Philosophy looks into the most important issues that face all of us.

Ethics is an area of philosophy that asks a very special question. What makes an action good or bad? This question comes up in all parts of our lives, and that includes the business world. In this course, we will talk about issues that affect you as a business person, as an employer or employee, and as a consumer.

What does it *mean* to do the right thing, in a business setting? *That* is the question that we will try to answer in this class.

Unit 1, Lesson 2

Exercise G

CD T-6 **Lecture Part III**

Female professor: Let me start out by giving you an example. Arden Textile is a company that makes sports clothes. I'm sure you have some of them at home — maybe you're even wearing them today. The company was started in 1906, and is still owned by the Arden family. In December 2003, a terrible fire destroyed the company's largest factory, and the company had to close. More than 1000 workers lost their jobs. The company's insurance paid for the loss. The Arden family talked about building a new factory overseas, where costs are lower. But instead they decided to rebuild the factory. During the rebuilding, the company gave all the workers their regular pay. This caused great financial problems for the company, and they almost went out of business.

Did the company do the right thing? Many people said yes, because Arden Textile helped their employees. The company president was on many TV programs, and received an award from the Prime Minister. But other people said no. They said that the main responsibility of a business is to make profits, and that's how it helps society the most.

We'll discuss this case in more detail next time. Your reading assignment is pages 5–27 in your textbook.

Unit 1, Lesson 4

Exercise A

CD T-7 **Professor 1:** OK, that's all for today. For next time, I would like you all to read chapters 7 and 8 of the textbook, and answer the questions on page 124.

Professor 2: Don't forget — your first writing assignment is due on Monday. You are to choose one of the topics and write an essay of 2–3 pages. If you have any questions about this, please come to see me in my office.

Professor 3: I have some homework for you over the weekend — it shouldn't take you very long, though. Please do exercises A, B, C, and D on page

53. You can write them in your notebooks — I'm not going to collect them, but we'll go over them in class on Monday.

Professor 4: If you'll look at your class schedule, you see that you have a listening assignment for Monday. You are to listen to CD number 2 of your course CDs. I know it's a long assignment, but I think you'll enjoy the music. Also, answer the questions on page 82 of your textbook. Have a good weekend!

Unit 2   Lesson 1

Exercise D

CD T-8 **Laura:** Hi, Jackie. I've been working all afternoon on this resume . . . What do you think?

Jackie: Let's see . . . OK, here's your contact information . . . What about your Web site? I think it's a good idea to include that.

Laura: Oh, I forgot about that! Now — what about the section on my education? It looks really short.

Jackie: Yeah . . . Well, you're a Spanish major, right?

Laura: Actually, my major is Spanish and Portuguese.

Jackie: You should definitely include that. And — where were you an exchange student?

Laura: In Brazil — in Sao Paulo.

Jackie: Put that down too. What year was that?

Laura: 2004.

Jackie: Hmm . . . The section on employment is kind of short too.

Laura: But I don't have much experience. That's my biggest problem.

Jackie: Maybe you should explain a little about each job. Like your job at the Cultural Society — what did you do there?

Laura: Oh, a lot of things. But mostly I wrote letters and e-mail in Spanish and Portuguese. And when they had special programs, I translated a lot of information on concerts and lectures.

Jackie: And what about the other job before that, what did you do there?

Laura: At the bank? Mostly a lot of computer work, but I also helped Spanish-speaking customers sometimes.

Jackie: Write something about that. And what about your volunteer work with the orchestra? What do you do there?

Laura: Well, when they have international guest

musicians who speak Spanish or Portuguese, I interpret for them. I take them around the city, things like that.

Jackie: That sounds fun! Now, let's see . . . if I were you, I would add another section. You could call it "Other Information."

Laura: Hmmm . . . What could I put there?

Jackie: Well, you lived in Mexico for a while, didn't you?

Laura: Yeah, that's right. You know my dad is Mexican — his company sent him to their Mexico City office, so we were there for four years when I was a kid.

Jackie: That must have been a great experience.

Laura: Yeah, it was . . . Hey, what about you? Have you found a job yet?

Jackie: Not yet, but I've applied for one that sounds really fun. A movie company is looking for someone to write the English subtitles for Spanish-language movies.

Laura: Wow, that sounds great! I hope you get it.

Jackie: Me, too!

Unit 2, Lesson 2

Exercise E

CD T-9

Interviewer: Good afternoon, Ms. Castro. I'm Rachel Carver, the Assistant Personnel Manager.

Laura: I'm pleased to meet you.

Interviewer: Now, first of all, can you tell me a little about yourself?

Laura: Well, I'm bilingual in English and Spanish. My father is Mexican and my mother is Canadian, and I grew up speaking both languages at home. My father's company transferred him to Mexico City when I was 14, so I went to high school there. Now I'm graduating with a degree in Spanish and Portuguese, and I really hope to use my knowledge of languages in my career.

Interviewer: That's a very interesting background. Can you tell me why you would like to join our company?

Laura: CreditPlus is one of the fastest-growing finance companies in North America, and the new Latin American branch is already very successful. I think your company has a very international perspective, and that's the kind of place that I would really like to work.

Interviewer: I'm glad to hear that. Now, why do you think you would be a good translator for us?

Laura: Well, I can give you two reasons. One is my language skills. I speak two languages that will be very important in the future. The second reason is my international experience. I spent a year in Brazil as an exchange student, and lived for four years in Mexico with my family. So I'm familiar with the cultures and customs of those countries.

Interviewer: Do you have any experience as a translator?

Laura: Yes, I do. I translated brochures and advertising at my summer job. I also translated e-mail messages for my supervisor.

Interviewer: Your background is very impressive. You'll be hearing from us.

Laura: Thank you very much for talking with me.

Unit 2, Lesson 5

Exercise B

CD T-10

Message 1: Hi Laura, this is Mark Johnson over here in the Marketing Department. I hope you have time to translate something into Spanish for me today . . . It's not very long, but we need it tomorrow. I hope that's OK with you. Anyway, it's a new ad that we would like to use in a business magazine in Mexico. It's just one page, so it shouldn't take you too long, right? Could you please give me a call?

Message 2: Hello Laura, this is Susan King in the company president's office. Are you very busy? We have a project for you, and I'm afraid it's a big one. We've just received a very important report, and it's in Portuguese. It's on banks in Brazil. The president would like to have it translated into English for a meeting on April 12 so that he can discuss it there. It's about sixty-five pages. Do you think you can do it by then? I can bring it to your office right away. Just give me a call. Thanks.

Message 3: Hello, this is Richard Black, the Director of Customer Service. We have a problem here, and I really hope you can help. We've written a letter for all our Spanish-speaking customers to tell them about the hours of our Spanish-language telephone service, and we need it translated. The service is only available until 5:00, and a lot of people call in Spanish in the evening and they can't understand when we explain. The letter is two pages long, and I've already e-mailed it to you. Thanks for your help!

Exercise A

CD T-11

Interviewer: Hello, and welcome to "Focus on the Arts." Our guest today is Jason Lee. He is the director of an international organization called Arts Unlimited. Mr. Lee is from Singapore, and this is his first visit to our country. Welcome to the program.

Jason: Thanks — I'm happy to be here.

Interviewer: Let me start out by asking about your organization, Arts Unlimited. What does it do?

Jason: Well, basically, we give advice to artists on how to sell their work more effectively. We help people develop programs for marketing art and crafts.

Interviewer: Where does Arts Unlimited operate?

Jason: We've developed programs in seven countries. I've been involved in our projects in Canada and Thailand.

Interviewer: Can you give us an example of these programs?

Jason: Sure! In Canada, we helped set up a Web site for people who make traditional crafts. As you know, Canada is a very big country, and a lot of artists live in remote areas. This Web site makes it possible for people to buy traditional crafts from the people who make them.

Interviewer: What are you going to be doing during your visit here?

Jason: Well, I was invited here by the Ministry of Culture. I'm going to have meetings with artists and craftspeople in different parts of the country. Together, we want to develop a plan for a national program to sell art to foreign tourists. The number of foreign visitors here has increased a lot in the last ten years, and we think this is a great opportunity for artists.

Interviewer: And are you an artist yourself, Mr. Lee?

Jason: Yes, in fact, I am. I'm a photographer. My specialty is nature photography, especially flowers and plants. While I'm here, I hope to take some time to visit your national parks and shoot lots of photos.

Unit 3, Lesson 2

Exercise A

CD T-12

Narrator: The Republic of Zimbaco is one of the world's newest nations. It became independent in 2002 but it has a long history. People have been living on this beautiful island for more than 3000 years. Today, the population is around 3 million people, and it is growing rapidly. Because we have very limited land for farming and little industry, we have to import many products from other countries. The cost of living is very high. Because of this, many traditional craftspeople have gotten jobs and have stopped producing crafts.

Zimbaco is divided into five provinces. Our capital, Zimbaco City, is located in the Northern Province on the coast and has a population of 750,000 people. The climate here is tropical, and many tourists come for vacations at one of our 53 beach resorts. Unfortunately, very few visitors go into the city to buy crafts. They spend most of their time at the beach. The most famous craft in this region is woodcarvings from tropical trees.

The Eastern and Southern provinces have a mild climate that is good for farming. The people like to decorate the outside of their houses with beautiful wall paintings. Now a group of about 80 craftspeople have begun selling boxes, dolls, and picture frames decorated with this traditional painting. This area is also famous for its traditional food, especially fruit and meat. These products must be refrigerated, though, so tourists don't like to buy them.

The Western Province is cut off by mountains. There are two small cities, but they can only be visited by boat. People in the region earn a living from fishing, and they also make beautiful crafts from shells.

The Central Province is 95 percent desert, with only about 50,000 people living in small villages. The desert people are famous for their beautiful pottery and weavings, which they have produced for centuries. However, the roads are poor and there are few facilities for tourists. Because of this, it's very difficult for craftspeople to earn a living there, and many of them are moving to the cities to get jobs.

Unit 3, Lesson 5

Exercise A

CD T-13

Team leader: Good morning, everyone, and thank you for coming here. We're meeting today for a very important reason. As you know, the government of Zimbaco has decided to spend $20 million dollars every year for new programs to support traditional art and crafts. This will do a lot to help the artists and craftspeople of our country. We have received proposals for fifteen different programs, and after careful studies, we have chosen the three best proposals. But there is only enough money to carry out one of these plans next year. Our objective today in this meeting is to decide which program to start next year. We're going to hear about the three programs, and then compare their advantages and disadvantages. First, I'd like to ask the director of the National Museum to tell us about . . .

Unit 4 Lesson 1

 Exercise E

CD T-14 **Emilie Duval:** Hello everyone, and welcome to our village of Saint-Marc. I'm so happy to see such a big group of volunteers, and I know we're going to have great summer together here.

Before I start talking about the program, I'd like to tell you a little bit about myself. My name is Emilie Duval, and I'm a Team Leader for Heritage Corps. I'm originally from the city of Toulouse, in the south of France, so I'm not far from home. Now I'm a fourth year student at the University of Paris, or rather I will be a fourth year student in September. My major is history, and I'm especially interested in France during what we call the medieval period, or the middle ages — the years 400 to 1400. I hope you will come to love it as much as I do.

This will be my third year with Heritage Corps here at Saint-Marc. The first year, I was an assistant to the archaeologists and I helped them make lists of all the objects they discovered. It was really interesting because that summer they were excavating the biggest house in the village. It's called the Le Blanc House, and it was the home of a rich family who sold wine. We found lots of dishes, keys, and even children's toys there. My second summer here, I helped to rebuild the walls of the house with stone. Now, this summer, our team is going to make the Le Blanc House into a visitor center that explains how people lived in the Middle Ages.

So, let me tell you a little about how our project is organized . . .

Unit 4, Lesson 2

 Exercise B

CD T-15 **Emilie Duval:** No one knows exactly how old Saint-Marc is. The earliest artifacts we've found are coins and pottery from the Roman times.

By the Middle Ages, it had become quite a large town, with about 3000 people. It was very wealthy because it was located in a rich wine-producing area. It had at least eight churches, and many streets of stone or wooden houses. Most of the houses had a shop on the ground floor, and the family lived upstairs. Wine from the region was sold as far away as Germany.

In 1458, an earthquake hit Saint-Marc. A number of the old stone buildings were destroyed, and people were afraid to live there. The earthquake also made the river dry up, and the town lost all its water. Life here became very difficult, and more and more people left the town. By 1700, all the buildings had been abandoned. Farmers let their cows and sheep use the area, and carried away some of the stones to use in new buildings. Most people in the area forgot that a large town had been here. In 1993 a professor at the University of Paris became interested in the site, and his students began excavating it. They were surprised to learn that Saint-Marc had once been the largest town in the area.

Unit 5 Lesson 1

 Exercise B

CD T-16 **Announcer:** You're listening to Radio International. And now, welcome to "Inside Education." This week our guest is Naomi Yoshida, an educational researcher who is looking at a very interesting question. Welcome to the program!
Naomi: Thanks. I'm very happy to be here.
Announcer: Could you tell us a little about your work?
Naomi: I'm with the Institute for Global Education, which is a part of Osaka University, in Japan.
Announcer: And what do you do there?
Naomi: Well, I'm a sociologist, which means I study how people live together in society. And my special field is comparative education — that's the study

of education in different countries. Right now, my institute is working on a project to compare people's ideas about schools in different countries.

Announcer: How are you doing that?

Naomi: Six of us researchers are going to different countries and asking groups of parents — and groups of students! — the same question: "What makes a good school?"

Announcer: That's a very interesting question!

Naomi: Yes, it is. And we're planning to collect information from twelve countries, and then analyze it to find similarities and differences.

Announcer: It sounds like a fascinating project.

Naomi: Oh, it is. I'll be visiting several cities in South Korea and Taiwan, and spending a month in each country. My colleagues will do interviews in a number of countries in Europe, Asia, and the Americas.

Announcer: And when will you have the answer to your question?

Naomi: Not for quite a while! We'll do all the interviews in the next few months, but it will take two years to put the results together and write our report.

Announcer: Well, we hope you'll come back and tell us about the results of your survey.

Naomi: I certainly will.

Unit 5, Lesson 3

Exercise F

CD T-17

Jae-Hak: I'm a student at an international school, and for me, a good school is one where there are all different kinds of students. They have different ideas and languages, but everyone is equal. At my school, some of the kids are foreign and some are Korean, but I have friends in both groups. My best friend is from China. My school is good because you learn how to get along with people who are different from you. I'm sure it will be useful for me in my future life.

Myoung-Hee: I'm lucky. I go to a nice modern high school that's only five years old, and we have new computers. But really, you can have a great school even in an old building. For me, the most important thing for a good school is the teachers, the way they teach and treat you. If they reward students for

good work and encourage you to try new things, you feel better about yourself and learn more.

Mrs. Shin: A good school is small enough that the staff know all of the children well. My daughter attended an elementary school with 2000 pupils! How can the teachers get to know them all? Then we moved to the country, and my son just started first grade in a school with only 300 children. There's such a difference. It's much more personal. Of course, there are some disadvantages, because the facilities aren't as good. But I'm very happy that my son is getting lots of personal attention, and he really likes his school.

Unit 5, Lesson 5

Exercise C

CD T-18

Social scientist 1: Yes, I'm having a very interesting stay. I'm doing a study of traditional religious customs here. This country is very modern in a lot of ways, but some of the elderly people still follow the old religion. People used to believe in nature gods and spirits. In my project, I want to find out how many people still follow the old customs. Tomorrow I'm going to the east of the country to talk to people there . . . What about you? Are you enjoying your time here?

Social scientist 2: My research is about changes in the system of government in this country in the last 20 years. Next week, I'm interviewing people in a lot of government departments to get their opinions about these changes — I'm asking them which changes are positive and which are negative. I'm sure I'll get some good information from them . . . What about you? What are you researching here?

Social scientist 3: You're right, Korea is a very important country for my work. You know, the economy here developed very fast after they started selling a lot of products overseas. I'm writing a book about why some countries earn a lot of money from exporting their products, but others aren't as successful. Maybe other countries can use these ideas to grow faster . . . And what about you? What do you do?